From Rags To Royalty

Preparing For Service In The King's Court

Connie Cenac

About the *Author*

Brothers, think of what you were when you were called. Not many of you were wise by human standards; not many were influential; not many were of noble birth. But God chose the foolish things of the world to shame the wise; God chose the weak things of the world to shame the strong. He chose the lowly things of this world and the despised things--and the things that are not--to nullify the things that are, so that no one may boast before him. It is because of him that you are in Christ Jesus, who has become for us wisdom from God--that is, our righteousness, holiness and redemption. Therefore, as it is written: "Let him who boasts boast in the Lord."1CO 1:26-31

When I became a radically saved Christian in 1980 at the age of thirty, I believed every word that came from the mouth of God; and I believed that my life must be spent to further His kingdom.

Even though I saw myself as very insignificant, I was faithful in church attendance, taught Sunday school, was a praise dancer for over ten years, and went on missionary trips from Europe to South America, to China and Africa. I even ministered in Holland every year for ten years, teaching people how to enter worship through dance. By most standards, I was fulfilling my divine destiny as a woman of God. I was very content in my church, and between managing our family business, taking care of our family, and ministry activities, was busy all of the time.

Looking back, I can see how God was eventually forced to uproot me from my comfort zone. After sixteen years in the same church, God ripped my heart out when He called my husband and me to leave our place of safety and venture into the unknown. Since then, God has led my husband and me into a place of leadership that we never ever desired. We have faced spiritual lions and tigers and bears—oh my

—and giants that chased us deeper into the heart of God—and into the plans and purposes of His eternal kingdom. It has been an adventure.

Pastoring the congregation at Sanctuary Church of Jacksonville and serving for 15 years on the Board of Directors at GoToNations—an international mission organization—has been a privilege and honor we never expected. In addition, as founders and President of the Board of Directors, we oversee the affairs of Seacoast Christian Academy, a fully accredited Christian school that takes care of children from infants to grade twelve—all of this, in addition to our responsibilities of managing our business affairs. Today, my podcast on YouTube and other social media channels—Connie's Corner—is reaching the world with the gospel of Jesus Christ! I am living proof that God chooses the foolish things of the world to confound the wise.

God has a plan for your life, too. Seek first His kingdom and His righteousness, and let God rock your life!

Table of Contents

Introduction

When Esther's were reported to Mordecai, he sent back this answer: "Do not think that because you are in the king's house you alone of all the Jews will escape. For if you remain silent at this time, relief and deliverance for the Jews will arise from another place, but you and your father's family will perish. And who knows but that you have come to royal position for such a time as this?"
-Esther 4:12-14

We are living in times of crisis, and our nation is at risk. Because our forefathers founded our country on the laws of God, we have been blessed with bounty and protected from our enemies. The last century brought a period of unprecedented wealth and prosperity. In spite of two world wars and other battles fought on foreign ground, we continued to prosper financially. But those days are over. The battle is no longer on foreign ground. The war is now waging on our very own land.

As a nation, we have turned our back on the God of the Bible—the Creator of the universe—the One who so richly blessed us. We have become a nation of blasphemers, greedy idolaters, child molesters, gluttons, drunkards, murderers, and sexual perverts. We give honor to the celebrities who lead our nation into debauchery, while we curse the holy Name of God on a regular basis. Though we elect our own government, we continue to choose men and women, who hate God and His ways, to lead our nation.

Worse than that, people who call themselves Christians go to church on Sunday and sleep around the rest of the week. Christian lawyers join in with the "wanna be a millionaire" club by assisting "victims" in legally robbing their fellow man for millions. Christian employees lie on their timesheets, enter into gossip in the workplace, and steal from their employers. Christian couples get divorced at a rate equal to or greater than their non-Christian counterparts.

Many pastors and televangelists have touched the gold and claimed the tithes and offerings as their own. They have built their big churches with their big administrative staffs and given themselves exorbitant salaries and tax-free housing allowances, leaving nothing for the widows, the orphans, and the aliens in their midst.

We have neglected God's word, and as a result, we have not taught our children the fear of the Lord, which is the beginning of wisdom. We have been unwilling to make the sacrifices necessary to keep our children out of the hedonistic public school system that leads our children astray; yet, we wonder why over 75% of all church-bred children end up falling into sinful lifestyles.

We are either too lazy or too busy to vote in general elections and allow the ungodly to rule our nation. We spend our time and our money to please ourselves. We act as if there is nothing we can do to halt the tide of evil in our nation—and so our nation is, indeed, at risk. God has been kind and merciful to us in spite of our spiritual adultery, but He will not be mocked. There is a price for sin, and we have certainly been storing it up for God's wrath. There is only one hope for the United States of America, and time is short. God is waiting for the church—not the denominational hierarchy or buildings, but the individual spiritual members of the church—to do what He commands in 2 Chronicles:

"When I shut up the heavens so that there is no rain, or command locusts to devour the land or send a plague among my people, if my people, who are called by my name, will humble themselves and pray and seek my face and turn from their wicked ways, then will I hear from heaven and will forgive their sin and will heal their land." -2 Chronicles 7:13, 14

In light of all of the tragedies surrounding the natural disasters affecting our nation—especially in the wake of hurricanes like Ivan, Katrina, and Rita; the forest fires and earthquakes in the west; flash floods and mud slides, to name a few—is it reasonable to assume that God has removed His mighty arm of blessing and protection from us in order to grab our attention?

The problem is that most Christians have been brainwashed into thinking that if they go to church, pay their tithes (and by the way, less that 25% of evangelical Christians even tithe), teach Sunday school, sing in the choir, and say prayers at mealtime, well, they've done their duty to God. Most people in the church believe that only those who wear the collar and get a paycheck from the church are called into full-time ministry. This faulty thinking is exactly why our nation is called a post-Christian nation today. The truth is, if you are a born-again Christian, you are called into full-time ministry—every last one of you! This is NOT a volunteer army, nor are we in the reserves—weekend warriors. We are all called to take up our weapons of warfare and get into the battle for the soul of our nation. The problem is that most of us are AWOL—absent without leave.

The purpose of this book is to open your eyes to the truth that you are as important to the salvation of souls and the rescue of this nation as Queen Esther was in her day, when she rescued the Jewish nation from annihilation. In addition, I hope to motivate you to prepare yourself for service in the King's court. How do you prepare yourself for royal service?

> *By taking a look at Esther,*
> *you will discover the qualities in her character that enabled God to use her in a spectacular*
> *performance that brought victory to her people.*

Throughout each chapter, you will find **Power Principles** that can change your life. At the end of each chapter, you will find points to ponder. These are questions designed to help you take the lesson of the chapter and apply it to your own life. I strongly encourage you to seriously consider and answer each question honestly and completely before moving on.

May God raise up an army prepared for full-time service in His royal court.

When he saw the crowds, he had compassion on them, because they were harassed and helpless, like sheep without a shepherd. Then he said to his disciples, "The harvest is plentiful, but the workers are few. Ask the Lord of the harvest, therefore, to send out workers into his harvest field."
- Matthew 9:36-38

CHAPTER 1

You Are *Unique*

Sixty queens there may be, and eighty concubines, and virgins beyond number; but my dove, my perfect one, is unique, the only daughter of her mother, the favorite of the one who bore her. The maidens saw her and called her blessed; the queens and concubines praised her. Song of Songs 6:8, 9

She was just a little girl when she came into stardom. She could sing, dance and act like no other child during those dreary depression days; but what really stole the heart of America was that little dimple that appeared on her face when she smiled. What made Shirley Temple so special? *She was unique!* There just wasn't any man, woman or child quite like her, and there hasn't been anyone since. Her movies gave hope to the hopeless and filled a need in the desperate lives of people struggling through trying times. Even today, she is still loved by men, women and children who long for the days when purity was in fashion.

Mary was a young virgin, engaged to a godly man, as was the custom of her day. She was born into the house of David during the Roman occupation of Judea. Times were really tough taxes were high, but her family was doing okay. Though they were among the poor, they were godly people who feared the Lord. She even had a relative who was serving in the temple in Jerusalem, that wonderful and beautiful holy city.

What a surprise— well actually, that's an understatement—what a shock it was to see the heavenly being appear in the garden. His words were like rivers of living water that filled Mary's heart with faith. In an instant, she was no longer a nobody from nowhere—she was to be the vessel that would bring into the earth the One so longed for. Messiah would soon be born to a virgin in Bethlehem, the City of David. What made Mary so special? She was unique! She was born into the right family at exactly the right time so that she might fulfill the purposes of God in the earth.

Joseph was the eleventh son born to Jacob—his father's favorite—and his brothers knew it. In fact, they didn't like him one iota. He had a special gift from God: he could interpret dreams. For instance, twice he dreamed that he would one day be in a position of authority over every member of his family. Well, that just wasn't acceptable to his brothers; after all, the eldest son was supposed to have that honor—certainly not the youngest one.

Many years later, after his own brothers betrayed and sold him into slavery and after he was falsely accused and sent to prison, Joseph was given the opportunity to use his gift to save the nation of Israel. Indeed, he did fulfill his dream and divine destiny when he became the second most influential man in Egypt—the most powerful nation of his day. What made Joseph so special? *He was unique!* He was born into the right family at exactly the right time, so that he might fulfill the purposes of God in the earth.

God has a special plan and purpose for your life as well.
He has strategically placed you exactly where you are today, so that you can fulfill
His purpose for your life.

You are unique!

Have you ever played a game of chess? If you have, then you know that each chess piece plays a special role. For instance, the pawns can only move one space forward at a time, except when they are needed to attack the opposition; in that case, they must move diagonally left or right one space. On the other hand, the queen can move unlimited spaces in every direction. If you want to win at chess, you need all the players because they protect the king.If you lose the king, you lose the game.If you understand strategy in the game of chess, you can begin to understand that God has a strategy for bringing about His purposes in the earth.

First we need to know what His purposes in the earth are. Although too many to mention, we'll just look at a few:

- God wants to reveal Himself to those who do not know Him.
- He wants every single person in the world to hear of His great love and mercy.
- He wants every sinner to come to the saving knowledge of Jesus Christ.
- He wants to transform lives so that people will walk in obedience to His royal law of love.
- He wants to set people free of evil spirits and strongholds of the enemy, so that people can experience His unlimited love and pass it around to other hurting people.
- He wants to bless people, especially the widows (single moms), the orphans, and the aliens in their distress.
- He also wants us to warn sinners of the coming wrath of God, so that they can come to their senses and repent.

In addition, God wants Christians to get in the game and play by His rules. He wants us to know Him intimately, so that we can experience His deep and enduring love towards us. He wants us to love those whom He loves—other people. He wants us to mature in our relationship with Him. He wants us to take up our cross daily and live a sacrificial life on behalf of others. He wants to take His place of authority in our hearts, so that we will live obedient lives that bring glory to His name. He wants His kingdom to come, His will to be done on the earth. That is what God wants. Is that what you want?

Power Principle #1
*You'll never fulfill God's purpose for your life
until you surrender your agenda in exchange for His agenda.*

You are vitally important in God's overall plan for the salvation of souls. What makes you so special? You are unique. That's the plain and simple truth. No one in the whole world is exactly like you. You were born into the right family at exactly the right time in order that you might fulfill the purposes of God in the earth.

In addition, God has blessed you with a physical body and a personality that has been designed just for you. He has also given you special talents that will equip you for service in God's kingdom. You are not a fluke of nature or a mistake. God wants you to know how special you are to Him. He says to you:

For I know the plans I have for you," declares the LORD, "plans to prosper you and not to harm you, plans to give you hope and a future. Jeremiah 29:11

There is a purpose for your life that has eternal consequences in your life as well as the lives of others.

Are you ready for service in the King's court?

You may be one of many in the church today who still believes the lies of the evil one. Maybe you come from a dysfunctional home, or were abused as a child, or lived a sinful lifestyle prior to coming to Christ. Maybe you still struggle with rejection, a spirit of abandonment, betrayal, anger, or some other stronghold in your life. You may even feel that you have nothing to offer in service to God. If you are a woman, maybe you have been told that only men can do this or that in the church. You may be deceived and believe that you must attend seminary or Bible college; or you must acquire the right college degrees or credentials; or you must be ordained by a mainline denomination in order to serve God.

If Jesus or His disciples are any indication of the truth, then we need to look at their résumés. Let's start with our Leader, the One we are called to follow:

Jesus Christ	Born in a manger in the little town of Bethlehem during the reign of King Herod
Parents	The Virgin Mary, of the house of David, and the Holy Spirit; earthly father was Joseph, the carpenter, also of the house of David
Education	At the feet of His mother, Mary, and earthly father, Joseph; the local synagogue; in close communion with His heavenly Father
Profession	Carpenter
Ministry	Preaching and teaching the good news of the kingdom of God, healing the sick, raising the dead, delivering the demoniacs, feeding the hungry, calming the storms, confronting religious leaders, etc.
Other Qualifications	Son of God, anointed by the Holy Spirit, passed the tests in the desert, compassion for those who were suffering, others too numerous to mention
References	Matthew, Mark, Luke, John, Paul, Mary, the 120 in the upper room on the day of Pentecost, over 500 saints on the day of ascension, and others upon request.

Levi	Also called Matthew, born somewhere in Judea during the Roman occupation
Parents	Son of Alphaeus, mother unknown at this time
Education	Disciple of Jesus of Nazareth, the Messiah
Profession	Tax Collector for the Roman government
Ministry	Spread the Gospel of Jesus the Christ, apostle to the church, wrote the Book of Matthew
Other Qualifications	Born again Christian, called by Jesus, anointed by the Holy Spirit on the day of Pentecost, surrendered to the will of God
References	Jesus of Nazareth, no others necessary

Simon	Called Peter, probably born in or near the town of Bethsaida of Galilee
Parents	Son of Jonah (great name for a fisherman)
Education	Disciple of Jesus of Nazareth, the Messiah
Profession	Fisherman, co-owner of family business with his brother, Andrew
Ministry	Spread the Gospel of Jesus the Christ, apostle to the church
Other Qualifications	Born again Christian, called by Jesus, anointed by the Holy Spirit on the day of Pentecost, surrendered to the will of God
References	Jesus of Nazareth, no others necessary

Andrew	Probably born in or near the town of Bethsaida of Galilee
Parents	Son of Jonah (great name for a fisherman)
Education	Disciple of Jesus of Nazareth, the Messiah
Profession	Fisherman, co-owner of family business with his brother, Simon Peter
Ministry	Spread the Gospel of Jesus the Christ, apostle to the church
Other Qualifications	Born again Christian, called by Jesus, anointed by the Holy Spirit on the day of Pentecost, surrendered to the will of God
References	Jesus of Nazareth, no others necessary

James	Called a son of Thunder, probably born somewhere near the Sea of Galilee
Parents	Son of Zebedee
Education	Disciple of Jesus of Nazareth, the Messiah
Profession	Fisherman, co-owner of family business with brother John
Ministry	Spread the Gospel of Jesus the Christ, apostle to the church
Other Qualifications	Born again Christian, called by Jesus, anointed by the Holy Spirit on the day of Pentecost, surrendered to the will of God
References	Jesus of Nazareth, no others necessary

John	Called a son of Thunder, probably born somewhere near the Sea of Galilee
Parents	Son of Zebedee
Education	Disciple of Jesus of Nazareth, the Messiah
Profession	Fisherman, co-owner of family business with brother James
Ministry	Spread the Gospel of Jesus the Christ, apostle to the church, took care of Mary, the mother of Jesus, after His death on the cross, wrote the Gospel of John, 1 John, 2 John, 3 John, and the book of Revelation
Other Qualifications	Born again Christian, called by Jesus, anointed by the Holy Spirit on the day of Pentecost, surrendered to the will of God, the disciple Jesus loved
References	Jesus of Nazareth, no others necessary

Philip	Probably born in or near the town of Bethsaida of Galilee
Parents	Unknown at this time
Education	Disciple of Jesus of Nazareth, the Messiah
Profession	Unknown
Ministry	Spread the Gospel of Jesus the Christ, apostle to the church
Other Qualifications	Born again Christian, called by Jesus, anointed by the Holy Spirit on the day of Pentecost, surrendered to the will of God
References	Jesus of Nazareth, no others necessary

Nathanael	Born in Cana of Galilee
Parents	Unknown
Education	Disciple of Jesus of Nazareth, the Messiah
Profession	Unknown
Ministry	Spread the Gospel of Jesus the Christ, apostle to the church
Other Qualifications	Born again Christian, called by Jesus, anointed by the Holy Spirit on the day of Pentecost, surrendered to the will of God
References	Jesus of Nazareth, no others necessary

We could go on, but none of the other disciples had much to brag about either.

*The number one credential for these ordinary men was that
they were disciples of Jesus Christ. Are you?*

We probably should look at the one apostle that did go to seminary, Saul, who later became Paul.

We probably should look at the one apostle that did go to seminary, Saul, who later became Paul.

Saul	Later named Paul, born in Tarsus of Cilicia
Parents	Jewish mother, don't know about dad, Roman citizen
Education	A Pharisee, thoroughly trained in the law of Moses under Gamaliel; had to be transformed under the teaching of the Holy Spirit
Profession	Tentmaker
Ministry	Spread the Gospel of Jesus the Christ, apostle to the Gentiles
Other Qualifications	Messianic Jew, called by Jesus, anointed by the Holy Spirit under the ministry of Ananias from Damascus, surrendered to the will of God
References	Jesus of Nazareth, no others necessary

Even Paul had a profession with which he used to support himself while he ministered to the churches throughout the Roman Empire. He had a real job—one with a paycheck. He didn't resign his position as tentmaker to preach the gospel or write a large portion of the New Testament. He worked hard so that he could be a blessing to the new churches that sprang up wherever he went.

However, let us examine Paul's life before Christ. He was a Pharisee who obeyed the letter of the law. As such, he was one of those who stood by and watched an innocent man named Stephen stoned to death. Though he had received a thorough education regarding the Law of Moses under the famous teacher, Gamaliel, he was an enemy of God who persecuted the church of Jesus Christ until he was transformed by the power of the Holy Spirit. So, what made Paul so special?

He was unique. He was born in the right place at exactly the right time; and he had the personality, the gifts and talents necessary to fulfill God's purpose in the earth at that time in history.

Every person on the face of the earth is unique and especially created for God's purpose. However, because of our sinful nature, we have been at war with God and brought pain, suffering and calamity rather than the blessing of God upon ourselves. It doesn't have to be that way. By the blood of Jesus and an act of our will, we can surrender our lives to the plan and purposes of God and become a vessel of honor and blessing in our day. We can become like Esther, who was born in the right place at exactly the right time to fulfill God's purpose in the earth.

Points to Ponder...

- Would you rather please God or yourself?
- Are you willing to do anything in order to fulfill God's plan for your life?
- Do you have a faith-based love relationship with God?
- Do you believe that God can use you to bless others?
- Do you see qualities in your character that can be useful in God's kingdom?
- Do you see unique talents that you can use for service in God's kingdom?

Quiet Time...

Dearest Heavenly Father,

Thank You for Your mercies that are new every morning. Thank You for the love that You poured out for me in the blood of Jesus Christ, Who took my sins, my sickness, my death, and my punishment upon Himself. Thank You for setting me free from the powers of darkness so that I can enter into an intimate relationship with You. Change my heart, oh Lord, and make me holy. Give me a passion to know You and a ravenous appetite for Your word. Reveal to me Your plan and purpose for my life, so that I might obey You and bring glory to Your holy name.
I love You, Lord. I am Yours, and You are mine. *Amen.*

But I have raised you up for this very purpose, that I might show you my power
and that my name might be proclaimed in all the earth.
Exodus 9:16

CHAPTER 2

The Plan of *Redemption*

Now there was in the citadel of Susa a Jew of the tribe of Benjamin, named Mordecai son of Jair, the son of Shimei, the son of Kish, who had been carried into exile from Jerusalem by Nebuchadnezzar king of Babylon, among those taken captive with Jehoiachin king of Judah. Mordecai had a cousin named Hadassah, whom he had brought up because she had neither father nor mother. This girl, who was also known as Esther, was lovely in form and features, and Mordecai had taken her as his own daughter when her father and mother died. Esther 2:5-7

Her mother and father had died, leaving Hadassah an orphan in a foreign land. This would have been tragic for the young Jewish virgin had she not been adopted by her God-fearing cousin, Mordecai. The Jews had been taken into captivity by the Babylonians years earlier, because God had turned His rebellious and idolatrous people over to their enemies. The Jewish people were now scattered throughout the Persian Empire, and Hadassah was among those living in the capital city of Susa.

One day, King Xerxes held a great banquet and wished to show off his beautiful wife, Queen Vashti. Unfortunately for her, she was not at all submissive to her husband. In fact, she refused his invitation to the banquet and brought shame to the king in front of his guests. As a result of this act of defiance, Vashti was dethroned and banished from the palace—while the king decided to find a new queen. Thus began the beauty pageant of the ages.

Hadassah was among the hundreds of beautiful young virgins who were taken from their homes throughout the kingdom and brought into the king's harem. Can you imagine how terrifying it must have been for this young Jewish girl to find herself in the harem of a pagan king? Put yourself into her shoes for just a moment.

First, Hadassah was taken out of her comfort zone. Her home was a place where she had been loved and protected from evil by her kind cousin, Mordecai. It was also a place where her Jewish customs were practiced—where family and friends gathered for food and fellowship—a place of joy and rest.

Hadassah was removed from her loving home to a place that was completely foreign to her; and she was required to live with other virgins who were waiting their turn to go to the king. If you know anything about women, you know that some can be vicious, especially when something as important as this is concerned. She would be one of very few, if any other, Jewish virgins living among pagan women who were involved in the disgusting idol worship of their own cultures. In other words, she would find little comfort among the company of the other young women.

What is even more devastating is that Hadassah would never know the warmth and love of a Jewish marriage and home. She would never again experience the wonderful celebrations and feast days that were a part of the daily life of the Jewish people. She would never again go with Mordecai to the synagogue, where she could listen to the rabbi teach about the wonderful promises of God's restoration for the nation of Israel. She would never again see her childhood girlfriends, nor would she ever again experience the loving comfort of her dear Mordecai. So much to lose…

Ponder further, if you will, her future if Hadassah was not the one chosen to be queen. Because a pagan king took her virginity from her, would she be destined to live out her lonely life without the love of a husband? What would her life be like living in the king's harem with so many other lonely concubines? Would there be any hope of happiness among so many unhappy, hopeless women? This young Jewish virgin, taken from her warm, loving home, was confronted with so many gut-wrenching questions as she was moved to a cold pagan palace.

God was in control.
He had a plan and a purpose for her life.
She was right where He needed her to be.

God's plan of the ages has always been to redeem that which was lost in the fall of Adam and Eve. As you recall, God had given Adam dominion over the earth and everything in it. He was God's ambassador, and so long as he obeyed God, everything would be terrific for every living creature. In fact, God told Adam to increase, multiply and fill the earth. It has always been God's will to fill the earth with His children, with whom He could have loving and intimate fellowship. If mankind had remained faithful to love and obey God, the earth would have never tasted sickness, poverty, war, calamity, or death. Unfortunately, we know it did not happen that way.

Adam joined in Satan's rebellion against God by choosing to disobey His direct command. The earth became cursed with sickness, death, murder, wars, famines, plagues, hatred, idolatry, and all the evil that comes from the rule of the prince of darkness—that diabolical devil, Beelzebub, none other than Satan himself. He is the absolute opposite of our loving God, and his rule is one of hatred and fear. His one purpose is to obtain what belongs to God—man's worship—and to sit on the throne as lord of the universe. In the meantime, he and his henchmen, the demons and fallen angels, work to destroy the souls of men and all that God created.

Ever since that sad day in the Garden of Eden, God has had a plan to deliver the earth and all that is in it from the powers of darkness and bring about the kingdom of God upon the earth. Where God governs and rules in the hearts of men, there is love, peace, joy and provision. There is life!

Satan is aware of God's plan of redemption that will bring about His kingdom of love on the earth, because God told him:

"And I will put enmity between you and the woman, and between your offspring and hers; he will crush your head, and you will strike his heel." Genesis 3:15

And so, the war between good and evil, light and darkness, life and death, heaven and hell, between God and Satan—the war of the ages began, with the winner taking all.

Little by little, God began to reveal His promise of redemption to those who feared His holy name. Out of all the peoples inhabiting the earth at the time, God found a man from Ur of the Chaldeans, an ordinary man, Abram, the son of Terah. He told Abram to pack up his bags, leave his comfort zone, his career, his house and business, his friends, his people, and his father's household and go to a land far away—a land of foreign people, one that God would show him. God promised him that:

"I will bless those who bless you, and whoever curses you I will curse; and all peoples on earth will be blessed through you." Genesis 12:3

Abram responded to the call of God and He led Abram and his family to the land of Canaan. Many people, who were not going to just sit there and let Abram take their land, inhabited this country. Imagine how Abram felt—what his thoughts might have been—when he arrived with his entourage and caravan to the place designated by the LORD. Looking over the land, with its many inhabitants, did he wonder if, perhaps, he had made a serious mistake when he left his own country? What on earth was he going to do in this land of promise? He was outnumbered. The inhabitants of Canaan could easily destroy him if they wanted to. God must have read Abram's mind, because the LORD once again appeared to Abram and said:

"To your offspring I will give this land." So he built an altar there to the LORD, who had appeared to him." Genesis 12:7

It was clear that Abram needed a word of encouragement—but this is something new! God tells Abram—who is already 75 years old, with no children of his own—that his offspring will inherit this land one day. And so, God's plan of redemption continues to unfold—a plan that will be fulfilled through the offspring of Abram. Satan must have believed it, because he immediately tried to derail God's plan by setting up Abram's wife for sexual involvement with another man.

There was a famine in the land, so Abram left Canaan and went down to Egypt to live for a while. As he was about to enter Egypt, he told his wife, Sarai:

"When the Egyptians see you, they will say, `This is his wife.' Then they will kill me but will let you live. Say you are my sister, so that I will be treated well for your sake and my life will be spared because of you." Genesis 12:12,13

Abram was right—when Pharaoh's officials saw that Sarai was a very beautiful woman, they praised her to Pharaoh, and she was taken into his palace. Before any damage could be done, God came to the rescue: He inflicted serious diseases upon Pharaoh and his household, and the message came out loud and clear. Pharaoh gave Sarai back to Abram, in addition: sheep, cattle, donkeys, servants and camels. Abram became a very wealthy man; and, what Satan meant for evil, God turned for good.

Later, after his nephew Lot had left Abram to live in the lush plains of the Jordan near the city of Sodom, the LORD made another promise.

He said to Abram: *"Lift up your eyes from where you are and look north and south, east and west. All the land that you see I will give to you and your offspring forever. I will make your offspring like the dust of the earth, so that if anyone could count the dust, then your offspring could be counted. Go, walk through the length and breadth of the land, for I am giving it to you." Genesis 13:14-16*

Satan is getting the message loud and clear. God is going to build a nation from this old man who doesn't have even one child to boast about. He must do something to stop it! Perhaps he can draw Abram into battle where his life can be snuffed out.

A war broke out, and the victors seized all the goods of Sodom and Gomorrah with all of their food. They also captured and carried off Abram's nephew Lot with his family and possessions, since he had been living in Sodom. When Abram heard about it, he called out the 318 trained men born in his household and went in pursuit of the enemy. During the night Abram divided his men to attack them, and he routed them, chasing them for a long distance. He recovered all the goods and brought back his relative Lot and his possessions, along with the women and the other people.

Incredible! Abram and his small band of men come back from the battle safe and sound, and Satan is foiled again. So, what could he do next?

> *What if Satan could get Abram to succumb to pride and greed?*
> *After all, these are all* ***idolatry!***

If Abram did succumb to pride or greed, he would fall under Satan's power, and the blessing of God would be removed from his life! Great idea! So, the devil sent the king of Sodom out to greet the returning hero. However, before the king can say anything to Abram, God sent Melchizedek, king of Salem and a priest of God Most High, who brought out bread and wine. He blessed Abram, saying:

"Blessed be Abram by God Most High, Creator of heaven and earth. And blessed be God Most High, who delivered your enemies into your hand." Genesis 14:19,20

Melchizedek's words reminded Abram that it was the LORD who had given him the victory over his enemies; so, as an act of worship, Abram gave the priest of God a tenth of everything *(So, that's where the tithe came from!)*.

When the king of Sodom offered to let Abram keep all the recovered goods for himself, Abram responded:

"I have raised my hand to the LORD, God Most High, Creator of heaven and earth, and have taken an oath that I will accept nothing belonging to you, not even a thread or the thong of a sandal, so that you will never be able to say, `I made Abram rich.' I will accept nothing but what my men have eaten and the share that belongs to the men who went with me--to Aner, Eshcol and Mamre. Let them have their share." Genesis 14:22-24

Satan lost another one! Abram had passed the test, and the word of the LORD came to him in a vision:

"Do not be afraid, Abram. I am your shield, your very great reward." Genesis 15:1

As you can see, Abram is a man of many colors. He is a man of faith, who leaves the safety and comfort of his home to follow God to a land he has never seen. However, when he finds himself in trouble, he leaves the land of promise and goes down to Egypt for provision. Fearful of the Egyptians, he places Sarai, his wife, in jeopardy to save his own life.

After God miraculously delivers him out of that situation, it seems that Abram is learning to trust God, as he shows great courage when he goes out to attack the four kings who had captured his nephew Lot. He passes the test of pride, when he gives God credit for his victory. He also passes the test of greed, when he refuses the wealth of Sodom, and instead, gives a tithe from his own wealth to Melchizedek. However, Abram is still a man who is struggling to understand the promise of God. Abram began to question God about the reality of His promise. Since he remained childless, he was beginning to wonder if his servant Eliezer of Damascus would inherit his estate. But the word of the LORD came to him, saying:

"This man will not be your heir, but a son coming from your own body will be your heir." He took him outside and said, "Look up at the heavens and count the stars--if indeed you can count them." Then he said to him, "So shall your offspring be." Abram believed in the LORD, and he credited it to him as righteousness. Genesis 15:4-6

Once again, God hears the questioning heart of Abram and makes it clear that he will have a son, one born of his own flesh—his offspring will be as numerous as the stars in the sky—and Abram believed the LORD.

Foiled again! Satan just could not win with this mighty man of God. So, he tried another route—his wife. We all know how Sarai, who was pretty old herself, became impatient with God and convinced her husband to have sex with her Egyptian servant, probably one who had come from Pharaoh's palace. Anyway, when Abram was eighty-six years old, Hagar indeed became pregnant and gave birth to Ishmael— and Satan must have thought he had won the victory!

However, thirteen years later, when Abram was ninety-nine years old, the LORD appeared to him again to confirm His covenant. He promised Abram that:

"You will be the father of many nations. No longer will you be called Abram; your name will be Abraham, for I have made you a father of many nations. I will make you very fruitful; I will make nations of you, and kings will come from you. I will establish my covenant as an everlasting covenant between me and you and your descendants after you for the generations to come, to be your God and the God of your descendants after you."
Genesis 17:4-7

God's plan continued to unfold, when God told Abraham that his ninety-year-old wife Sarai would bear the child of promise:

God also said to Abraham, "As for Sarai your wife, you are no longer to call her Sarai; her name will be Sarah. I will bless her and will surely give you a son by her. I will bless her so that she will be the mother of nations; kings of peoples will come from her." Abraham fell facedown; he laughed and said to himself, "Will a son be born to a man a hundred years old? Will Sarah bear a child at the age of ninety?" And Abraham said to God, "If only Ishmael might live under your blessing!" Then God said, "Yes, but your wife Sarah will bear you a son, and you will call him Isaac. I will establish my covenant with him as an everlasting covenant for his descendants after him.

And as for Ishmael, I have heard you: I will surely bless him; I will make him fruitful and will greatly increase his numbers. He will be the father of twelve rulers, and I will make him into a great nation. But my covenant I will establish with Isaac, whom Sarah will bear to you by this time next year." Genesis 17:1522

What a surprise it must have been for both Abraham and Sarah. They had given up all hope of having a son of their own. They had bypassed the plan of God, by bringing forth a son through Hagar the Egyptian; as a result, they had already suffered much jealousy and grief. Despite their actions, God was going to honor His word and give them a son who would be the heir of the covenant.

Now, even Satan realizes that the promise of redemption will indeed come through Sarah. No way! She's ninety years old! Impossible! In this battle between life and death, Satan once again must take action. If he can defile Sarah, by having her sexually involved with a man other than her husband, the word of God would be broken, and the victory would be his. Apparently, fearful of the inhabitants of the land, Abraham once again told the people that Sarah was his sister rather than his wife. This time, Abimelech king of Gerar, took her into his home. Once again, God supernaturally intervened:

But God came to Abimelech in a dream one night and said to him, "You are as good as dead because of the woman you have taken; she is a married woman." Now Abimelech had not gone near her, so he said, "Lord, will you destroy an innocent nation? Did he not say to me, `She is my sister,' and didn't she also say, `He is my brother'? I have done this with a clear conscience and clean hands." Then God said to him in the dream, "Yes, I know you did this with a clear conscience, and so I have kept you from sinning against me. That is why I did not let you touch her. Now return the man's wife, for he is a prophet, and he will pray for you and you will live. But if you do not return her, you may be sure that you and all yours will die." Genesis 20:3-7

Can you believe it? Abraham, the great man of faith, continues to show cowardice towards the inhabitants of the land. Despite his shortcomings, God remains faithful to Abraham: God's promise came to pass, and Sarah became pregnant. She bore a son to Abraham in his old age, at the very time God had promised him.

Abraham was one hundred years old when his son Isaac was born to him.

Abraham was a man who feared God, but his greatest test of faith came years later when he was asked by God to offer his son, Isaac, on the altar as a sacrifice. I am sure that the hordes of hell were gathered to see if this man would choose to disobey God and nullify his covenant with God. It seemed that God was really pushing this obedience thing.

Abraham had a long time to think about his decision during the three-day journey it took to reach the place God had told him about. He could have changed his mind and taken his beloved son, Isaac—the one he had waited one hundred years for—back to his camp, but he didn't. He obeyed God. After he built an altar, he bound his son Isaac and laid him on the wood. As he lifted the knife to slay his son, an angel of the LORD called out to him from heaven and said:

"Abraham! Abraham!" "Here I am," he replied. "Do not lay a hand on the boy," he said. "Do not do anything to him. Now I know that you fear God, because you have not withheld from me your son, your only son." Genesis 22:11,12

God provided a ram in the bush for the sacrifice, and Isaac's life was spared. God had found a man whose heart belonged completely to Him. The angel of the LORD called him a second time and said:

"I swear by myself, declares the LORD, that because you have done this and have not withheld your son, your only son, I will surely bless you and make your descendants as numerous as the stars in the sky and as the sand on the seashore. Your descendants will take possession of the cities of their enemies, and through your offspring all nations on earth will be blessed, because you have obeyed me." Genesis 22:16-18

As you can see, God's plan of the ages is unfolding—a plan that is based upon His promises and our obedience.

> **Power Principle #2**
> *The blessing of God upon our lives is the direct result of our obedience.*

We can fast forward to the promise God made years later to Isaac's own son. When Jacob left his father and mother to find a wife among his relatives in Haran, God confirmed His covenant in a dream:

"I am the LORD, the God of your father Abraham and the God of Isaac. I will give you and your descendants the land on which you are lying. Your descendants will be like the dust of the earth, and you will spread out to the west and to the east, to the north and to the south. All peoples on earth will be blessed through you and your offspring. I am with you and will watch over you wherever you go, and I will bring you back to this land. I will not leave you until I have done what I have promised you." Genesis 28:13-15

Up until this time, Jacob's relationship with the God of his fathers had been superficial, at best. He now has an encounter of his own with the Living God, who promises that:

- God will give Jacob and his descendants the land of promise.
- Jacob's descendants will be as numerous as the dust of the earth—that is more than can be numbered.
- All of the peoples and nations on earth will be blessed through Jacob and his offspring.
- God will watch over Jacob, wherever he goes.
- God will return Jacob to the land of promise.
- God will not leave Jacob until He has accomplished all that He has promised.

These promises from God, written on Jacob's heart, would carry him for many years to come, as he experienced great sorrow and suffering before his return home to the land of promise.

Later in life, Jacob and his family are led into Egypt during a famine, where his son Joseph has been placed in a position of great honor and authority. His family is given a place to settle down and prosper. It even seems that they may never leave this rich real estate and return to the land of promise. Wouldn't that make the devil happy! God's word would be broken and all would be lost!

Before Jacob dies, he calls his sons together to bless them. As he places his hands on the head of Judah, he proclaims:

"Judah, your brothers will praise you; your hand will be on the neck of your enemies; your father's sons will bow down to you. You are a lion's cub, O Judah; you return from the prey, my son. Like a lion he crouches and lies down, like a lioness—who dares to rouse him? The scepter will not depart from Judah, nor the ruler's staff from between his feet, until he comes to whom it belongs, and the obedience of the nations is his. Genesis 49:8-10

Jacob prophetically identifies the royal bloodline that will bring forth the promised Messiah—the Lion of Judah—who will one day rule the nations. As God's plan continues to unfold, Satan continues in his pursuit to destroy the very people who will bring his own destruction! Satan is at war, and the Jewish people are caught in the middle!

As the centuries pass, Satan manipulates his puppets to bring destruction to God's people. You know, people like Pharaoh, who enslaved the Hebrews and required that they kill their newborn sons. That did not work, so he enticed the Israelites to rebel against God in the desert. That slowed things down a bit—about forty years. But then there was that faithful man, Joshua, who led the children of Israel into the land of promise. When the walls of Jericho fell, Satan just about had a heart attack; so, he enticed Achan to disobey the command of God: he took plunder from the city and hid it for himself. As a result, the Israelites were defeated in the battle at Ai.

> *The battle continued throughout the centuries, as Satan lured the people of God to bow down and worship the gods of the nations that surrounded them*

Their disobedience and idolatry aroused the anger of God, Who turned them over to their enemies. They would repent, and God would restore them. Over and over, like a broken record, the people of God would repeat the mistakes of their ancestors—until there was no end to their rebellion. And so, it looked like Satan had won the war.

Nebuchadnezzar, king of Babylon—who completely destroyed Jerusalem and the temple of God—overtook the nation of Israel. Men, women, and children—the young and the old, the strong and the feeble—died from famine, plague, and sword. Only a remnant lived to tell about the destruction, and most of them were carried off into exile. Years later, the Babylonian kingdom was given to the Medes and the Persians.

The remnant of God's people were strangers in a foreign land when Satan pulled out his wild card. He had an ambassador in the palace of King Xerxes: his name was Haman the Agagite. All the royal officials at the king's gate knelt down and paid honor to Haman at the king's command; but Mordecai would not kneel down or pay him honor.

Points to Ponder...

- Do you see the faithfulness of God throughout history?
- Do you see the spiritual battle between God and His enemies?
- Have you taken the time to read the Old Testament?
- Do you hunger for a deeper understanding of God and His ways?
- Are you willing to change your priorities in order to know the God of the Bible?

Quiet Time...

Dearest Heavenly Father,

I long to know You and Your ways, oh Lord. I want to be a vessel You can use in the battle between the kingdom of God and the powers of darkness. I have filled my life with so much activity, that I have failed to spend time in Your word. Please help me prioritize my life to make room for You. Help me to overcome my love for this world, so that I can be an obedient servant in Your courts of love. I love You, Lord. I am Yours, and You are forever mine. *Amen.*

For he has rescued us from the dominion of darkness and brought us into the kingdom of the Son he loves, in whom we have redemption, the forgiveness of sins.
Colossians 1:13,14

CHAPTER 3

The Day of *Preparation*

"Go, consecrate the people. Tell them, `Consecrate yourselves in preparation for tomorrow; for this is what the LORD, the God of Israel, says: That which is devoted is among you, O Israel. You cannot stand against your enemies until you remove it.' Joshua 7:13

When King Xerxes' order and edict had been proclaimed throughout the kingdom, many girls were taken from their homes and brought to the royal city of Susa. Once they arrived at the palace, they were put under the care of Hegai, who had charge of the harem. Esther (Hadassah's Persian name) was also taken to the king's palace and entrusted to Hegai. Because she won his favor, he immediately began her beauty treatments and provided her with special food. In addition, he assigned seven maids from the king's palace to attend to her and moved them into the best place in the harem.

Meanwhile, Esther's cousin Mordecai walked back and forth near the courtyard of the harem to see how she was doing and what was happening to her. Because Mordecai had forbidden her to do so, Esther did not reveal her nationality to anyone in the palace. And so, she prospered in the harem of the king.

Each young girl was required to undergo twelve months of preparation, prior to her turn to go to King Xerxes. For six months, she would receive treatments with oil of myrrh, and then six more months with perfumes and cosmetics. When the time came for her to go to the king, she was given anything she wanted to take with her from the harem to the king's palace. When her turn came, she would go to the king in the evening, and in the morning, she would return to another part of the harem—to be placed under the care of Shaashgaz, the king's eunuch who was in charge of the concubines. Unless the king was pleased with her and summoned her by name, she would never return to the king. She would simply live out her remaining years as one of many lonely women in the harem of the concubines.

Imagine all that was going through the mind of Esther—a young Jewish virgin among so many other beautiful young women, all of them in the prime of their youth. Who would be chosen to be queen? Why would God allow one of His own to be defiled by a pagan king? How could this possibly be His will? Hadn't He forbidden His people to intermarry with pagans? Wouldn't He want Esther to marry a nice young Jewish man, so that together they might bring forth children for His kingdom? None of this made sense—at the moment. And so, the time arrived.

When the turn came for Esther (the girl Mordecai had adopted, the daughter of his uncle Abihail) to go to the king, she asked for nothing other than what Hegai, the king's eunuch who was in charge of the harem, suggested. And Esther won the favor of everyone who saw her. She was taken to King Xerxes in the royal residence in the tenth month, the month of Tebeth, in the seventh year of his reign. Esther 2:15,16

Esther's future rested in the hands of God, and He always leads His people to victory, never to defeat. Esther was prepared for service in the King's court.

Now the king was attracted to Esther more than to any of the other women, and she won his favor and approval more than any of the other virgins. So, he set a royal crown on her head and made her queen instead of Vashti. And the king gave a great banquet, Esther's banquet, for all his nobles and officials. He proclaimed a holiday throughout the provinces and distributed gifts with royal liberality. Esther 2:17,18

Can you imagine the celebration in the hearts of Mordecai and Esther? Surely, they were giving thanks to the Lord God Almighty, Who had lifted this Jewish orphan into a place of honor and influence. God is not a respecter of persons, for He had done for this young woman the same thing He had done for Joseph in Egypt and Daniel in Babylon. Yes, God can even use women for His plan and purpose in the earth. He can use anyone who is prepared for service in the King's court, and that includes you.

There is a time of preparation for every occasion, no matter how insignificant. We can see this in our daily activities. For instance, before we go to work, we must groom and dress ourselves. We don't just jump out of bed and into the car—we prepare ourselves for the day.

When a huge event such as a wedding is planned, we may take months preparing for the big day. There are invitations to be sent out, ordering the cake, purchasing the bridal gown and tuxedos, reserving the church and banquet facilities, choosing the wedding party, planning the reception dinner and dance, and a multitude of details that must be taken care of before the big day. Preparation is the key to success.

> *In God's plan of redemption,*
> *He uses obedient servants who have been prepared for the occasion.*

Although every young virgin in the harem was beautiful, and each of them received the same beauty treatments, only Esther was chosen. What made her so special? *She was prepared for service in the King's court.* Her *character* set her apart from the rest of the royal beauties. Not only was she lovely to look at, she was also a beauty on the inside. In addition to her regal robes, Esther was clothed in *humility*, the first requirement for service in the King's court.

```
Power Principle #4
Humility is the first requirement for service in the King's court.
```

First and foremost, if you are to be a queen in the King's court, you must be humble and submissive like Esther. The Bible says:

But Esther had kept secret her family background and nationality just as Mordecai had told her to do, for she continued to follow Mordecai's instructions as she had done when he was bringing her up. Esther 2:20

Even though Esther had been elevated to royalty as queen, she remained **humble**, and submitted herself to the counsel and instruction of her cousin Mordecai. Can you imagine that? Here she was, the Mrs. Universe of her day. She was Queen of Persia! She could have gotten a little puffed up with pride. After all, she was chosen from among all of the young, beautiful women of her day. And yet, she did not think so highly of herself, nor did she imagine herself wiser than the person who had raised her up as a child. Unlike the deposed Vashti, Queen Esther maintained a submissive spirit in spite of her highly esteemed position in the palace. She was neither puffed up with pride nor arrogant in her approach with others.

Humility and a submissive spirit are two sides of the same coin. Only a humble person will submit herself to anyone else, including God and His royal law of love. A proud person will never fulfill God's plan and purpose for her life.

Let us take a closer look at *pride*. *Pride* is defined as *"inordinate self-esteem"*. A proud person is haughty, arrogant, insolent, and disdainful. In other words, pride causes a person to exaggerate his or her own self-worth or importance, thus placing self in the seat of honor, power, and authority.

Pride is self-reliant and independent, in need of no other, including God. An independent person:

- is not subject to the control of others;
- does not rely on anyone or anything else;
- does not look to others for guidance in conduct.

Does this describe anyone you know? Well, the sad truth is, there are a lot of people in the church today who are like this. From pastors in the pulpit to the people in the pews, pride stealthily infiltrates the hearts of those who are called to humility. Is it possible that those who hide in the pews of big churches is hoping that no one will hold them accountable or require anything of them? Is there any wonder that the church in America has missed the mark despite her best efforts, and we as a nation are no better off than Sodom and Gomorrah? The only way to pull our nation out of her deep sin is for the church to repent of pride and seek humility. Then we will fulfill God's purposes for our nation. God's word warns us: *The Lord detests all the proud of heart. Be sure of this: They will not go unpunished. Proverbs 16:5*

God hates pride.
Do you?

Pride goes before destruction, a haughty spirit before a fall. Proverbs 16:18

The wicked Haman, the man closest to the king of Persia, was such a man. Filled with pride and inordinate self-esteem, he became the enemy of God and an instrument of Satan in his attempt to thwart God's plan of redemption.

After these events, King Xerxes honored Haman son of Hammedatha, the Agagite, elevating him and giving him a seat of honor higher than that of all the other nobles. All the royal officials at the king's gate knelt down and paid honor to Haman, for the king had commanded this concerning him. But Mordecai would not kneel down or pay him honor. Esther 3:1,2

The stage is set for the battle to begin, and God is in control.

Points to Ponder...

- How are you doing on the scale of humility?
- Are you submissive in your marriage, or do you have to argue every issue with your spouse?
- Are you respectful of your parents, the elderly, or those in positions of authority?
- Do you seek counsel when making major decisions?
- Do you see yourself as wise beyond your years?
- Can you acknowledge that you are not the ultimate authority on most issues of life?

Quiet Time...

Dearest Heavenly Father,

Lord, I confess that humility is not one of my strong points. In fact, for some reason, I seem to think I can make decisions apart from the counsel of Your word. Please forgive me for allowing pride to rule my life. I confess that I am a desperate person and apart from You, I can do nothing of eternal value. Show me the foolishness of my ways and help me walk in humility all the days of my life. Help me become more like Jesus, who humbled Himself, when He left the glories of Heaven to live a life of humility, even to the point of death on a cross. I need You, Lord. I am Yours, and You are mine forever. ***Amen.***

Seek the LORD, all you humble of the land, you who do what he commands. Seek righteousness, seek humility.
Zephaniah 2:3

CHAPTER 4

The *Conspiracy*

Then the royal officials at the king's gate asked Mordecai, "Why do you disobey the king's command?" Day after day they spoke to him but he refused to comply. Therefore, they told Haman about it to see whether Mordecai's behavior would be tolerated, for he had told them he was a Jew. Esther 3:3,4

Queen Esther's cousin, Mordecai, was a man of wisdom, courage, and integrity. In obedience to the Law of Moses, he would not bow down to honor Haman, nor anyone else other than the Lord God Almighty. Rather than fall in with the crowd, he chose the favor of God over the favor of man. Because he was unwilling to compromise his convictions in order to be politically correct, he risked persecution by those in authority. His act of courage was the fuel Satan needed to stir up hatred for the Jewish people.

Unfortunately, it is the same today. When God's people speak the truth, it stirs up hatred and persecution against the true church of Jesus Christ. That is exactly why Christians are tortured and murdered in most parts of the world today. It has always been that way.

Satan has used this tactic so effectively that many Christians keep their mouths shut over issues that really matter. Who cares if our country is going to hell in a hand basket? We often sit silently while the wicked corrupt our nation with their filth and lies. There are pastors who are fearful of speaking the truth from the pulpit, because they might lose their tax exemption status, or someone in the pew may be offended. Meanwhile, there are Christians who continue in their sinful lifestyles, fornicate, get abortions, divorce each other, and vote for politicians who hate God and His ways. God's word warns us:

You adulterous people, don't you know that friendship with the world is hatred toward God? Anyone who chooses to be a friend of the world becomes an enemy of God. James 4:4

Power Principle #5
The Kingdom of Darkness or the Kingdom of God.
You choose

Back to our story, Haman was enraged when he saw that Mordecai would not kneel down to pay him honor. But killing Mordecai was not enough! There had to be a way to destroy all of his people, the Jews, throughout the kingdom of Xerxes. Haman found a way and unknowingly entered into a conspiracy with Satan to thwart God's plan of redemption.

Then Haman said to King Xerxes, "There is certain people dispersed and scattered among the peoples in all the provinces of your kingdom whose customs are different from those of all other people and who do not obey the king's laws; it is not in the king's best interest to tolerate them. If it pleases the king, let a decree be issued to destroy them, and I will put ten thousand talents of silver into the royal treasury for the men who carry out this business." Esther 3:8,9

The King's most trusted advisor tells him that there are people in all the provinces of his kingdom who do not obey the king's laws. This was not true; but then, Satan always uses deception to bring people to ruin. In this case, the deception of Haman convinces the king to allow him to destroy the Jews. As a result, the king took his signet ring from his finger and gave authority to Haman to *"do with the people as you please." Esther 3:11*

The royal secretaries were summoned, and they wrote out all of Haman's orders to the king's governors over the various provinces, and the nobles of the various peoples, in the script and language of each people. They were written in the name of the King himself and sealed with his own ring. These orders were sent out to all of the king's provinces by couriers, with the order to destroy, kill and annihilate all of the Jews— men, women, children, young and old—on a single day, the thirteenth day of the twelfth month, the month of Adar. They were also given permission to plunder their goods. A copy of the edict was to be issued as law in every province and made known to the people of every nationality, so that they would be ready for that day.

The couriers went out spurred on by the king's command, and the edict was issued in the capital city of Susa. Satisfied with his success, Haman sat down with the king to relax with a drink. Satan's plan appeared to be infallible. The remnant of Jews scattered throughout the kingdom of Xerxes would be destroyed in one day! God's plan of redemption would be over. Finished. Undone. The kingdom of darkness wins. Satan's rule over the affairs of men is forever settled.

Can you imagine how the Jews must have felt when the news arrived in the towns and provinces where they had been living peaceably for many years? Scattered and unarmed, they were to be like sheep led to the slaughter. Their babies, their old parents, the helpless—all alike, were to be killed in one day! Surely, they responded the same way that Mordecai did, when he learned of all that had been done. The only difference was that he knew who the culprit was—the one who had orchestrated their destruction was that vile Haman!

When Mordecai learned of all that had been done, he tore his clothes, put on sackcloth and ashes, and went out into the city, wailing loudly and bitterly. But he went only as far as the king's gate, because no one clothed in sackcloth was allowed to enter it. In every province to which the edict and order of the king came, there was great mourning among the Jews, with fasting, weeping and wailing. Many lay in sackcloth and ashes.
Esther 4:1-3

When Esther heard about Mordecai from her maids and eunuchs, she was greatly disturbed. Something must be terribly wrong for her cousin to go about in sackcloth and ashes. So, she sent him some clothes to change into, but he would not accept them.

Then, she sent Hathach, one of the king's eunuchs assigned to her, and ordered him to find out what was going on with Mordecai—why on earth he was in mourning.

When Hathach found him in the open square in front of the king's gate, Mordecai told him everything that had happened, including the exact amount of money Haman had promised to pay into the treasury for the destruction of the Jews. In addition, he gave him a copy of the edict, which had been published in Susa, to show to Esther. He instructed Hathach to urge Esther to go into the king's presence to beg for mercy and to plead with him on behalf of her people.

When Esther received Mordecai's message, she sent this message back to him: "*All the king's officials and the people of the royal provinces know that for any man or woman who approaches the king in the inner court without being summoned the king has but one law: that he be put to death. The only exception to this is for the king to extend the gold scepter to him and spare his life. But thirty days have passed since I was called to go to the king.*" Esther 4:11

When Mordecai received Esther's message, he sent back his reply:

"*Do not think that because you are in the king's house you alone of all the Jews will escape. For if you remain silent at this time, relief and deliverance for the Jews will arise from another place, but you and your father's family will perish. And who knows but that* **you have come to royal position for such a time as this***?*" Esther 4:13,14

Power Principle #6
God's timing is perfect.
He is never caught off guard!

Esther was, indeed, placed in her royal position by the hand of God for such a time as was necessary to fulfill God's divine plan of redemption. But—the big question remained—would she do her part? Like martyrs throughout the centuries, would she be willing to risk everything—her royal position, her life of luxury, even her own life —in order to fulfill her divine purpose?

God knew what He was doing when He chose a young orphan girl named Hadassah to fulfill a heroic role in the battle between the hordes of evil and the Kingdom of God. She was born in the right place, at exactly the right time, to fulfill her divine destiny.

Points to Ponder...

- Are you generally politically correcting in your thinking?
- Are you afraid to speak up in defense of others?
- Are you willing to make yourself accountable to others?
-
- Are you willing to take risks for the sake of the Kingdom of God?
- Are you willing to take risks on behalf of others?
- Given one choice, would you choose to please God or other people?

Quiet Time...

Dearest Heavenly Father,

Thank You for Your love and Your mercies that are new every morning. I sure do need them. Sometimes I am afraid to speak the truth, even when I know it is the right thing to do. I confess that many times I am concerned about what others think of me. Please deliver me from the fear of man and replace it with the fear of the Lord. I would rather please You than have the praises of men. Change my heart, oh Lord, and make me holy. May the meditations of my heart and the thoughts of my mind be pleasing in Your sight, oh Lord. I love You. I am Yours, and You are forever mine.
Amen.

Hear me, O God, as I voice my complaint; protect my life from the threat of the enemy. Hide me from the conspiracy of the wicked, from that noisy crowd of evildoers.
Psalms 64:1,2

CHAPTER 5

The Character of *Nobility*

A wife of noble character who can find? She is worth far more than rubies. Her husband has full confidence in her and lacks nothing of value. She brings him good, not harm, all the days of her life. Proverbs 31:10-12

I f you are a true child of God, then you have been born into the ultimate *royal family*. We are joint heirs with Jesus Christ, the King of kings and the Lord of lords, and we have an inheritance found in the riches of His kingdom. If we are to be found faithful among the brethren, then we must cultivate the qualities in our life that are of **noble character.**

Power Principle #7
*Our **character** determines what we will do— whether we will live to please ourselves or live to fulfill God's purpose for our lives.*

Esther was a woman of **noble character** who fulfilled her divine destiny and saved the nation of Israel from annihilation—the nation that would bring forth the Savior of the world, Jesus Christ.

Esther was asked by her cousin Mordecai to intervene with the king to save the lives of her countrymen throughout the Persian Empire. She could have chosen to remain silent and politically correct—after all, she was the queen! She could have closed her eyes to the impending disaster and loss of life. She could have said, "Well, you know, it *is* against the law for me to go to the king without his invitation. Surely, you don't expect me to put my life in danger for a bunch of people I don't even know!" But Esther could not just sit by and do nothing. Her message to Mordecai says a lot about her **character:**

Then Esther sent this reply to Mordecai: "Go, gather together all the Jews who are in Susa, and fast for me. Do not eat or drink for three days, night or day. I and my maids will fast as you do. When this is done, I will go to the king, even though it is against the law. And if I perish, I perish." Esther 4:15,16

Look closely and you will see the humility and the courage of this great queen. First of all, Esther was not a lone ranger. She was a team player, and she required that all of the Jews in the kingdom fast with her. Because of her **humility**, she knew that she could not carry the burden alone. She also understood the power of **spiritual unity**.

You cannot fulfill your divine purpose without the help of others.

We must be willing to unite with other believers who are serious about God. Now, I am not just talking about going to church every Sunday and sitting in the pew. I am talking about relationship and commitment. The church is not an organization, although that is what some have become. It is a living organism made up of individual living cells—that's you and me. Like the human body, each and every cell is transparent and ministers in some way to the rest of the body. **Spiritual unity** can only occur in this kind of church. Remember, God is not impressed with one-man shows —he uses the body of Christ, as we walk together with one purpose in the spirit of unity.

Now we know that the purpose of fasting is to accentuate our prayer life; so, in effect, Esther was seeking the favor and direction of God, another quality found in a **humble** heart. She was not going to depend on her own ability to influence the king to change his mind: she was completely reliant upon the love and faithfulness of God to deliver her nation from annihilation.

> *Esther was **unselfish**.*
> *She could have remained silent and politically correct— she was, after all, safe from harm in the King's palace.*

Remember, the king had been manipulated by Haman to sign an edict that would allow all of the Jews scattered throughout the Persian Empire to be slaughtered on a particular day. The only Jew who had access to the king was Esther, his wife. But even she could not approach the throne without first being summoned by the king. To violate this protocol was cause for death. Esther was in quite a predicament.

Now, imagine yourself in her place. Esther has completed the three days of fasting and prayer, and it is time for action. She calls for Hagai, the eunuch in charge of the harem, and asks for his assistance. While assisting with her royal robes, he tries to talk her out of this dangerous violation of royal protocol, but she is a woman on a mission—committed to the task at hand. She walks from the queen's quarters to the royal court, her heart pounding—her life hanging in the balance—she is a woman of *courage*.

> *Esther was a woman of **courage**, willing to take risks on behalf of others.*
> *She was willing to lay down her life in order to fulfill her divine destiny.*

Courage is rare in our day. We are a nation whose faith in God has been crushed, and fear now motivates many Americans to do what they do. Many Christians are polarized by the fear of man. They are ineffective in their witness and afraid to step out of their comfort zone. Fear will keep you from fulfilling your divine destiny. There is only one antidote to fear, and that is a faith-based intimate love relationship with Jesus Christ.

> *Courage* is a by-product of faith in the love and faithfulness of God and His word.

That is why a Jewish orphan girl could eventually place her life on the line for her people.

On the third day Esther put on her royal robes and stood in the inner court of the palace, in front of the king's hall. The king was sitting on his royal throne in the hall, facing the entrance. When he saw Queen Esther standing in the court, he was pleased with her and held out to her the gold scepter that was in his hand. So, Esther approached and touched the tip of the scepter. Esther 5:1,2

God was with Esther, and her life was spared.

> **Power Principle #8**
> *If God sends you into the lion's den, you won't go in alone.*

Now, we know from the rest of the story that Esther did not just fall at his feet begging for mercy for herself and her people, isn't that what most of us would have done? Or, she could have cried out, "Xerxes, what have you done? Why didn't you ask me first, before you went and signed that ridiculous proclamation? I know that I failed to tell you that I am a Jew, but this thing you have done is really stupid!"

Okay, we would never say such a thing to our own husbands, would we? No— and thank God, neither did Esther, who instead had prepared a battle plan for her mission. *Wise* beyond her years, she planned her approach to the king very carefully, giving time for God to do His thing. Esther was a *wise* woman, who thought before she spoke.

Then the king asked, "What is it, Queen Esther? What is your request? Even up to half the kingdom, it will be given to you." "If it pleases the king," replied Esther, "let the king, together with Haman, come today to a banquet I have prepared for him." "Bring Haman at once," the king said, "so that we may do what Esther asks." Esther 3-5

Now, imagine the king sitting on his throne among all of his nobles. Standing in the doorway is his beautiful young wife dressed in all of her royal splendor. He wonders, *"What could she possibly want from me that she would risk her own life. It must surely be a critical issue, and yet, she simply invites us to dinner. Why doesn't she just ask? I'm willing to give her anything her heart desires, up to half of the kingdom! Why doesn't she just ask? Why the dinner invitation?"*

> *Esther sets the stage for God to do His thing.*
> *Rather than pressing the matter, she prepares*
> *her husband to hear her heart.*

So, the King and Haman went to the banquet Esther had prepared. After dinner, while the king was relaxing with a goblet of wine, he asked her again:

"Now what is your petition? It will be given to you. And what is your request? Even up to half the kingdom, it will be granted." Esther 5:6

Esther is once again promised up to half the kingdom, if it was her desire. You know, she could have stopped there. She could have decided that she liked being the queen, and half the kingdom isn't a bad split of assets. The fact is, Esther was once again tested and found to be ***unselfish***, she was not out for number one.

> *Satan basically promised Jesus the same thing—just bow down and worship me, and I'll give you*
> *all of the kingdoms of this world. Jesus passed the test, and so did Esther.*
> *Would you?*

Esther was also a very **patient** woman, who allowed God time to rewrite history. Once again Esther invited them to dinner. She replies:

"My petition and my request is this: If the king regards me with favor and if it pleases the king to grant my petition and fulfill my request, let the king and Haman come tomorrow to the banquet I will prepare for them. Then I will answer the king's question." Esther 5:7,8

With her answer, Esther has set the stage for God's supernatural intervention in the affairs of men.

You, too, can be a stagehand in the reality show of the ages, when you choose to trust in God's eternal and unfailing love.

Haman left Esther's banquet very happy and in high spirits, but on the way home, he saw Mordecai sitting at the king's gate. When he neither rose nor showed fear in his presence, Haman was furious. Nevertheless, he restrained his anger and went home.

When he arrived at his house, he called his wife, Zeresh, and his friends and bragged to them about his great wealth, his many sons, and how he'd been elevated over all of the other nobles and royal officials by the king. His pride was bursting from within him when he boasted that:

"I'm the only person Queen Esther invited to accompany the king to the banquet she gave. And she has invited me along with the king tomorrow. But all this gives me no satisfaction as long as I see that Jew Mordecai sitting at the king's gate." Esther 5:12,13

Haman's wife and friends came up with a deviously clever idea. They told him to have a gallows built that would be so tall, everyone in the city would be able to see it. Then, in the morning, he should go and ask the king to have Mordecai hanged on it. Afterwards, he could go with the king to the banquet with a happy and satisfied heart. The suggestion seemed good to Haman, so he had the gallows built seventy-five feet high.

> *Timing is everything.*

God knows exactly what He's doing all of the time! Surely, He causes all things to work together for the good of those who love Him and are about His business.

That very night, the king was having a bout of insomnia inspired by God Himself. The king ordered that the history books, especially the record of his reign, be brought in and read to him—good reading for insomniacs. Esther's **patience** was paying off. During the reading, it was found recorded that Mordecai had saved the king's life, when he exposed a plot by two of the king's guards to assassinate him. When the king asked if Mordecai had received any special honor or recognition for his deed, his attendants told him that nothing had been done for him.

Obviously, the king wanted to do something for this courageous man who had saved his life, so he asked his attendants if there was anyone hanging out in the court. They told him that Haman had just entered the outer court of the palace. He had actually come to ask the king about hanging Mordecai on the newly built gallows prepared for him. The king ordered that Haman be brought to him.

When Haman entered, the king asked him, "What should be done for the man the king delights to honor?" Now Haman thought to himself, "Who is there that the king would rather honor than me?" So, he answered the king, "For the man the king delights to honor, have them bring a royal robe the king has worn and a horse the king has ridden,

---

one with a royal crest placed on its head. Then let the robe and horse be entrusted to one of the king's most noble princes. Let them robe the man the king delights to honor, and lead him on the horse through the city streets, proclaiming before him, `This is what is done for the man the king delights to honor!'" Esther 6:6-9

The king commanded Haman to go at once and do all that he had suggested for Mordecai the Jew, who sits at the king's gate. Things are heating up, and guess who's stoking the fire—God! Esther's patience is beginning to bear fruit, and she isn't even in charge.

If God is for you, who can be against you? You plus God are a majority.

> *Power Principle #9*
> *The victory is yours when you allow the battle to belong to God.*

God does have a sense of humor, you know. Haman is a perfect picture of Satan in his effort to destroy all of the Jews. His hatred of Mordecai led him to conspire to kill all of the children of God alive at that time. Satan was simply using him to thwart God's promise of a Jewish messiah in the person of Jesus Christ. Now Haman finds himself in a terrible predicament.

After Haman obeyed the king's command to honor Mordecai, he ran home devastated. When he told his wife and friends all that had happened, they warned him of what he already knew—Mordecai was a Jew—and Haman was doomed. They were still talking when the king's eunuchs arrived to take him to the banquet that Esther had prepared.

So the king and Haman went to dine with Queen Esther, and as they were drinking wine on that second day, the king again asked, "Queen Esther, what is your petition? It will be given you. What is your request? Even up to half the kingdom, it will be granted." Esther 7:1,2

Esther's **humility** flowed from her heart in her **respectful** approach towards her husband. Listen to her heart and the words that she uses to convey such a critical issue when she answers the king:

Then Queen Esther answered, "If I have found favor with you, O king, and if it pleases your majesty, grant me my life--this is my petition. And spare my people-this is my request. For I and my people have been sold for destruction and slaughter and annihilation. If we had merely been sold as male and female slaves, I would have kept quiet, because no such distress would justify disturbing the king." Esther 7:3,4

Can you imagine that? If the Jews had only been sold into slavery, she would not have bothered her husband; but, slaughter and annihilation, well, that's a horse of a different color. Esther was also very **respectful** in speech. She was not a nag who had worn out her husband with trivial complaints; so, when she had something extremely important to tell him, he was ready to listen.

> *Because of her wise and humble attitude toward her husband, Esther now has his full attention.*

King Xerxes asked Queen Esther, "Who is he? Where is the man who has dared to do such a thing?" Esther said, "The adversary and enemy is this vile Haman." Esther 7:5,6

Things are heating up and guess who's in the pot! Haman was terrified, and the king left the room in a rage! While the king went out into the garden, Haman, realizing that the king had already decided his fate, stayed behind to beg Queen Esther for his life.

Just as the king returned from the palace garden to the banquet hall, Haman fell on the couch where Esther was reclining. The king exclaimed, "Will he even molest the queen while she is with me in the house?" As soon as the word left the king's mouth, they covered Haman's face. Then Harbona, one of the eunuchs attending the king, said,

"A gallows seventy-five feet high stands by Haman's house. He had it made for Mordecai, who spoke up to help the king." The king said, "Hang him on it!" So, they hung Haman on the gallows he had prepared for Mordecai. Then the king's fury subsided. Esther 7:8-10

Power Principle #10
*Give God room to move on your behalf,
and you will see the mighty brought low and the humble lifted up!*

That very day, King Xerxes gave Esther the estate of Haman. In addition, he gave Mordecai the king's signet ring, which he had reclaimed from Haman. Although the king could not reverse the edict to kill the Jews in all of the provinces of his kingdom, he gave Mordecai and Esther the authority to write another decree in the king's name on behalf of the Jews.

And so, the edict went out throughout the kingdom of Xerxes, giving the Jews the right to assemble and protect themselves; to kill, destroy, and annihilate any armed force of any nationality or province that might attack them, and to plunder the property of their enemies. For the Jews, it was a time of joy, gladness, and honor. Wherever the edict was proclaimed, there was feasting and celebration, and the fear of the Jews seized the hearts of their enemies.

When the appointed day arrived, the Jews assembled in their cities to attack those seeking their destruction. The governors and king's officials helped the Jews, because they were afraid of Mordecai, whose reputation spread throughout the provinces. They struck down their enemies with the sword, killing and destroying those who hated them. In the city of Susa, they also killed the ten sons of Haman and hanged them on the gallows.

Without lifting a finger against her adversary, Esther rescued a nation from annihilation—all because she was truly a woman of noble character!

King Xerxes imposed tribute throughout the empire, to its distant shores. And all his acts of power and might, together with a full account of the greatness of Mordecai to which the king had raised him, are they not written in the book of the annals of the kings of Media and Persia? Mordecai the Jew was second in rank to King Xerxes, preeminent among the Jews, and held in high esteem by his many fellow Jews, because he worked for the good of his people and spoke up for the welfare of all the Jews. Esther 10:1-3

Points to Ponder...

- What are you doing to further the kingdom of God?
- Are you walking in intimate fellowship with other Christians who are living their lives for the purposes of God?
- Have you chosen to forfeit your own plans in order to fulfill God's plans?
- Are you willing to risk your life to save others?
- Are you willing to suffer long and allow God the time to change the hearts and minds in the lives of those you love?

Quiet Time...

Dearest Heavenly Father,

You are so awesome! When I see Your mighty hand at work on behalf of Your children, my heart leaps for joy, for I am confident that You will move mountains for me, as well. Lord, I want to be a vessel You can use to set the captives free. Purify my heart and fill me with Your unconditional love for others. Give me an undivided heart, that I might live to please You, my Lord and my King. I love You. I am Yours, and You are forever mine. *Amen.*

Lift up your heads, O you gates; be lifted up, you ancient doors, that the King of glory
may come in. Who is this King of glory?
The LORD strong and mighty, the LORD mighty in battle.
Psalms 24:7,8

CHAPTER 6

The *Hiding Place*

The LORD is my rock, my fortress and my deliverer; my God is my rock, in whom I take refuge. He is my shield and the horn of my salvation, my stronghold. I call the LORD, who is worthy of praise, and I am saved from my enemies. Psalms 18:2,3

I f you are passionate for God, then you are a candidate for a position of holy power in the army of God. He is still seeking true worshippers—people like Queen Esther, Joseph, and Daniel—who will lay down their own plans, hopes and dreams in order to serve the King of the universe. The real tragedy, however, is that many in the church who truly love God never fulfill their divine purpose in the earth. How can that be? The problem may be ***strongholds.***

Webster says...

Stronghold:
  1. *a place of ¡security or survival;*
  2. *a fortified place;*
  3. *a place dominated by a particular group*

We all come into God's kingdom with strongholds of various kinds. Some are self-inflicted, some are the result of hurtful or destructive actions against us, while others are placed in our hearts by the father of lies—you know who! A stronghold of the enemy in our hearts will cause us to make wrong choices and fall short of God's will for our lives.

For example, I once had a stronghold of the enemy called "unworthy". It all came about when I was five years old. It was a bright and beautiful Christmas morning, when I took my "new" bicycle outside. My mother held me up, while I took my first lesson in riding. It didn't take long to realize that my bicycle was different from all of the others on the block. It seemed that every kid on my street got a bright, shiny new bike for Christmas. Mine, however, was way too big for me and had dents and rust on it.

My dad was a shift worker in the local nylon plant, and my mother stayed home with her three small children. Because finances were tight, my Christmas bicycle was purchased second hand from the newspaper ads. Somehow, the deceiver spoke to my 5-year-old heart and convinced me that I was not worthy of having a bicycle like the other children had. A seed of "unworthiness" took root in my heart. By the time I was 19, I thought no one else would ever love me: so, I married my first husband, the wrong person, at the wrong time, for all the wrong reasons. Nine years and plenty of mistakes later, we ended in divorce.

Satanic strongholds usually begin during childhood, mostly through negative or hurtful events in our lives. Something happens to us that wounds our hearts, and a seed of deception is planted by our adversary, the devil.

I once had a stronghold of fear in my life. I was scared to death of speaking or doing anything in front of an audience. When I became a praise dancer in church at the age of thirty-four, I would pray for an hour before each service in order to get the courage to join the procession into the sanctuary. Even then, I would make a mad dash to the restroom right before services began, because my stomach was not cooperating with me. One day, while speaking with a friend, I told her about my fears—and suddenly, God revealed the source of those fears:

It began when I was ten years old. While playing my accordion during a recital, I forgot my notes and embarrassed my mom and dad. Then, when I was 13, I tried out for cheerleader at Brownsville Junior High School in Pensacola, Florida. When I finished my cheer with a jump, I slipped on the freshly waxed stage and landed on my bottom in front of the whole student body. Embarrassing as that was, I stood up without crying and did my cheer over again. Unfortunately, I did not make the squad. If that wasn't enough, at the age of 14 while marching in the school drill team in front of an audience of 7,000 people, I mistakenly stood on the wrong yard line and messed up the entire half-time show!

From that point on, I believed myself to be a complete buffoon and failure—no way was I going to put myself in that position ever again! At least, not until God pulled that weed out of my heart. As I shared these stories with my friend, God instantly set me free from the fear of man. I am no longer afraid of anyone and am free to be a fool for Christ!

If seeds of deception take root in our hearts, then we end up making serious decisions in life based upon lies. Our choices are made, not in accordance with the will of God, but under the influence of the kingdom of darkness. Jesus gives us a description of the devil:

"He was a murderer from the beginning, not holding to the truth, for there is no truth in him. When he lies, he speaks his native language, for he is a liar and the father of lies."
John 8:44

Satan's number one weapon of mass destruction is deception. When people believe the lie, they will always make wrong choices and offend God. Imagine that you are on a road trip, and you have been given a map that will take you from Miami, Florida to Anchorage, Alaska. The map is correct, and you have chosen a route that will get you to your destination. The only problem is, someone wants to deceive you and decides to take all of the road signs along the path and mix them all up. Your trip will be filled with confusion, and you will end up somewhere that you never intended.

So, it is with our lives. God has given us a road map with directions on how to live a victorious life—one that ends up in the right place. The kingdom of darkness blinds us to the truth that will lead us to make right decisions that bring blessing to us and to those that we love. That is why Jesus said:

"I am the way and the truth and the life." John 14:6

He also said that the truth shall set you free—free from satanic strongholds—free to live a life that is pleasing to God.

Some strongholds are the result of our own defense mechanism. For instance, at the age of thirteen, while on a hayride with friends, I was kissed by a boy for the first time in my life. It came as a shock at first, but he won my teenage heart. When he later broke up with me to go back to his old girlfriend, I was devastated! For months, I could not eat or sleep. I even had thoughts of suicide over him! Can you imagine how I felt when it happened again a year later? Once again, I fell head over heels over another boy—and again, he broke up with me to go back to an old girlfriend. Rejected for the second time, I made up my mind right then that I would never allow a boy to make me cry again.

That soul vow became a stronghold—a defense mechanism meant to protect me from ever having a broken heart again. Those walls also kept my first husband out of my heart—and I was unable to love him as a wife should love her husband. In fact, I was not able to love any man until the curse of that vow was broken by Jesus. It took some time, but eventually, He walked right through those walls and set me free to love everyone from the heart!

Today, I love my husband, Dwight, unconditionally, and we are truly one in the spirit. It wasn't easy for either of us—heart surgery is painful, you know—but the results are heavenly.

> *If you could only taste and see that*
> *The fruit of love is delicious and worthy of any price.*

Some strongholds are the result of lies perpetrated by others. My husband, Dwight, is a perfect example. When he was only six, his mother divorced his father, who was a heavy drinker and a chronic gambler. After she remarried two years later, Dwight never saw his real dad again. He was told that his father had decided not to interfere with his new life—and so, Dwight went through life believing the lie that his dad did not love him. A spirit of abandonment and rejection tormented him his entire life, causing him to experience one destroyed relationship after another, which only added to his hurt and rejection.

It took many years and the unconditional love of his praying wife to bring Dwight to a place of complete healing and deliverance. Just recently, after the death of his mother, we found documents and pictures that revealed an entirely different story than the one he had been told. The truth is that his father died of a broken heart. His postcards and letters revealed a man who loved his family, and specifically his little son, deeply. He may have had a problem with gambling at the time, but he paid child support until Dwight reached the age of 18. He did not abandon Dwight but sent letters reaching out to him—letters that he never saw until now. How sweet the truth is—my husband has finally found peace with his past, and a new anointing is flowing from him in service to the Lord.

Maybe your father or mother lied to you, too. Maybe they told you that you were no good, would never amount to anything, that you were stupid or lazy—don't believe it for a second. God doesn't make junk! Believe the truth, it's in His love letter to you.

He has already decreed:
You are a pearl of great price and worth the greatest ransom ever paid for a captive victim— the
blood of Jesus!

Some strongholds are the result of physical or sexual abuse during childhood. For instance, most homosexual men were molested as children or teens.

A friend of mine is the mother of two tall, blonde, and handsome identical twins. When they were sixteen years old, one of the twins left home and hitchhiked to south Florida to see his father. On his way to Miami, a man picked him up and molested him. Devastated, he returned home and took up a homosexual lifestyle. However, his identical twin, raised in the same home under exact circumstances, has remained heterosexual. Explain that! One of the teens believed the lie that is perpetrated through the media and the public-school doctrine: he was born that way. How is that possible, when the identical twins were born with the same set of genes? It isn't—but you won't hear that from the experts.

What happens to a child who is molested by an adult? We must remember who the real culprit is—the enemy is an unseen devil who works through a broken, thoroughly wounded and depraved human being—one that has also been taken captive and enslaved to sin. The curse of that sin is passed on to the victim through deception. Unless the child immediately tells an understanding, adult and forgives the perpetrator, the curse will take root in the heart of the child—and the cycle continues. That is why the sin of the father passes on to the next generation.

The only hope for the victim of physical or sexual abuse is a life-changing intimate relationship with the Great Physician. Jesus is the antidote for sin and its consequences.

> *Jesus was the victim of physical and sexual abuse as he was beaten and crucified naked on a wooden cross.*

Most lesbians and prostitutes were molested as children. For example, beginning at ten years of age, a friend of mine was molested by her father every night. As a teen, she lived a life of promiscuity, became pregnant, and gave her child up for adoption. When she married sometime later, she and her husband became believing Christians. Together, she and her husband pastored a small, but growing church. Their four children were prayer warriors and well versed in the Bible. They were the perfect Christian family—until she left home to live a lesbian lifestyle.

How could this happen to a woman who had led many others into a life-changing relationship with Jesus? The fact is, she had never been set free of the stronghold that held her captive to her past. Yes, she loved the Lord. Yes, she wanted to serve God. Yes, she had a call on her life to pastor others. However, she had never been healed of the wounds inflicted upon her soul by her own father. She talked about her past and even used her testimony to lead others to the Lord, but the curse had never been broken. Oh, how must it grieve the Lord to see one of His own dragged back into the pit. This is why Jesus warned against this kind of abuse when He said:

But if anyone causes one of these little ones who believe in me to sin, it would be better for him to have a large millstone hung around his neck and to be drowned in the depths of the sea. MT 18:6

Many women have been abused by husbands or boyfriends and are captive to a root of bitterness that causes them to hate men. They are unable to enter into true intimacy with their husbands, and they go from one relationship to another, adding insult to injury. It does not have to be that way.

Another dear friend of mine was molested by her father her entire life, beginning at the age of three. Today, she has a passionate love for the Lord and for her husband. She told me that she forgave her father, especially when she found out that he, too, had been molested and abused as a child. She decided to dwell on the sacrifices her father had made on her behalf while she was growing up. She chose to love her father unconditionally, and today, he is also living for the Lord. What a testimony of the power of God to change lives.

Many men and women in the church today are captive to generational curses. The husband of a dear friend once told me his story:

He and his sister and brother were raised by alcoholic parents—and I mean really drunk, all of the time, alcoholics. If it were not for the mercy and generosity of neighbors, they would have starved to death. They lived in abject poverty and actually slept outside on the porch of their run-down shack every night.

Today, his brother and sister are alcoholics, following in the footsteps of their parents. I asked my friend if he could explain why he turned out to be a well-adjusted, happily married devoted husband and father. His answer is exactly what I expected. He said that his brother and sister condemned his parents and would not forgive them for all of the suffering they endured because of their alcoholic lifestyle. On the other hand, he had chosen to love his parents in spite of their lifestyle and forgave them for all they had done. This explains why Jesus warned us:

"Do not judge, and you will not be judged. Do not condemn, and you will not be condemned. Forgive, and you will be forgiven. Give, and it will be given to you. A good measure, pressed down, shaken together and running over, will be poured into your lap. For with the measure you use, it will be measured to you." Luke 6:37,38

In other words, you reap what you sow. If you sow mercy towards others, you will receive mercy in your life. If you sow judgment towards others, you will reap judgment in your own life. In the same measure that we give to others, whether mercy and forgiveness or judgment and condemnation, we will reap a harvest of the same.

When we refuse to forgive the person who has hurt us, we bring a curse on our own lives. The key to freedom from this kind of generational curse is forgiveness. It unlocks the shackles that keep us in bondage to our past. It also sets the offender free to experience the mercy of God.

Because of the generational curse of greed in my husband's family, Dwight, like his father, was captive to gambling. Prior to our marriage and his surrender to the Lord, Dwight would go into a casino expecting to leave a winner. Because he is a genius with numbers, he did win at blackjack on a regular basis: but, when he tried the dice at the craps table, he was hooked. He was like the proverbial fish that took the bait and became dinner for the devil. I stood by helplessly and watched him squander thousands of dollars every time he walked into a casino. Until one night, after losing more money than I could count…

We were leaving the casino when I asked him, "Dwight, are you coming back tomorrow night?" He answered, "Yes." I said, "So, are you going to win?" He said, "Yes." I answered him, "I bet that is exactly what your father told your mother!" That night, at that very moment, light broke through the darkness in his heart: Dwight realized that he had become his father. It was the first step towards his deliverance.

Although Dwight was able to stop gambling through self-discipline, the demons constantly tempted him whenever we were near a casino. It was several years later while sitting in church that the Holy Spirit convicted him of greed, which is idolatry. His heart broke over the truth of his sin, and he repented right then and there. As a result, he has never since had a desire to gamble again.

The generational curse of gambling was broken over my husband by the power of God, when he was willing to repent of his sin of greed, the root cause of gambling. Unfortunately, his sister never repented, and she became a thief who spent time in and out of prison for stealing time and time again.

Dwight is fulfilling God's plan and purpose for his life today, because he is truly free to love others. He has been transformed by the power of God to love me, to love others, and to live a life that is pleasing to God. Hallelujah!

Some strongholds are the result of our own sins. For example, a man turns on his computer to find a pornographic web advertisement staring him in the face. He is tempted to take a peek—surely there is nothing wrong with a little peek. I mean, after all, he loves his wife, but she hasn't been very loving to him lately. No big deal.

Power Principle #11
Pornography is poison, and poison kills.

68

Jesus once said:

"You have heard that it was said, `Do not commit adultery.' But I tell you that anyone who looks at a woman lustfully has already committed adultery with her in his heart." Matthew 5:27,28

So, when this mystery man takes a peek at that porn site, he is willfully disobeying the commandment of God that speaks of adultery. He has opened his heart to a spirit of lust and perversion that will lead him to do unspeakable things, even to those whom he loves. Many people captive to the disgusting spirit of lust have molested children. In addition, wives have been forced into perverse sex, because their husbands have been given over to a perverted spirit of lust and a depraved mind.

Lust is a familiar spirit *(a demon spirit)* that acts as a magnet and attracts others with the same spirit. It does not matter how pretty or ugly, skinny or fat, rich or poor you are, you are attractive and attracted to anyone with a spirit of lust. The truth is lust is ugly, evil and disgusting! It is the devil's counterfeit for God's incomparable and unconditional love. There is only one way to be set free from the power of lust— repentance and forgiveness. The apostle Paul tells us to:

Flee from sexual immorality. All other sins a man commits are outside his body, but he who sins sexually sins against his own body. 1CO 6:18

Flee from sexual immorality, that means, turn around and run as fast as you can to get away from its tentacles! You need to see lust as God sees it: it makes Him want to throw up. I really believe that, if people completely understood the reality that God sees everything and knows every detail hidden in our hearts, we would not want Him to see us do some of the things that Christians do in the dark!

Some strongholds are the result of a wrong teaching or belief system. What we believe determines what we will do. For instance, if I believe that my pregnancy is nothing but a blob of tissue with no spirit or soul, or that it has no feelings, no emotions, nor purpose, what is wrong with abortion? However, the word of God says something different.

"Before I formed you in the womb I knew you, before you were born, I set you apart; I appointed you as a prophet to the nations." JER 1:5

If I believe that God knows every person before they are even formed in the womb, and that God has set each person apart for a special purpose, then I will see abortion as murder.

If I believe that abortion is murder, then I will do whatever is within my power to put an end to it. I will help with crisis pregnancy centers, if possible. I will write letters to congressmen, and I will vote for men and women who will defend the lives of unborn children, regardless of party affiliation. If I believe that God hates abortion and grieves over every murdered baby, then I will certainly not ever have an abortion or vote for someone who supports abortion.

You see, this one belief—that abortion is murder—sets in place actions that please God. However, if I believe the lie, and I choose to abort my baby, then I rebel against God and set in motion a whole new set of actions that will bring a curse on my life. One such woman, Carol Everett, talks about her life as an abortionist in her book, *Blood Money—Getting Rich off a Woman's Right to Choose*. Without a college education, she made a fortune from the over 35,000 abortions she **sold** to unsuspecting women. She shares how it all began, when her own husband threatened her with divorce if she did not abort their baby. Like so many women today, she made the wrong choice and killed her baby. Sadly, her marriage ended in divorce anyway. Praise God for his mercy—she came to a life-changing relationship with Jesus who set her free from the spirit of greed that held her captive to the sin of murder. God is awesome!

Our actions will either please God and bring blessing into our lives, or they will offend God and bring a curse upon our lives. If what we believe determines what we will do, then how do we defend ourselves against deception? It is very important that we believe the truth of God's word. That is why the Apostle Paul says:

The weapons we fight with are not the weapons of the world. On the contrary, they have divine power to demolish strongholds. We demolish arguments and every pretension that sets itself up against the knowledge of God, and we take captive every thought to make it obedient to Christ. 2 Corinthians 10:4,5

We have all been brainwashed from birth by the father of lies, that devil who brings confusion even to believers. We must ensure that our thoughts are the same as God's thoughts as outlined in His word. We must take captive every thought that exalts itself above the word of God. The truth of God's word is our only defense against the lies of Satan.

We must also protect our children from the lies of the enemy, because there is no such thing as a harmless lie. What are your children learning in school? If they are in a public school, they are learning that there is no God, or that all gods are equal—we must be tolerant. They are learning that humans are an accident of nature and part of the "evolving" animal kingdom. I even heard that lie when I was in school, but God's word says something entirely different: God created man in His own image and gave him dominion over the animal kingdom—not what the evolutionists and environmentalists teach. They are also learning that homosexuality is an acceptable lifestyle—I guess it is to the intellectual elite, but God's word says that it is an abomination to Him. Oh, yes, I must mention, our children are learning that it is right and normal to be sexually active at any age outside of the context of marriage. Is it any wonder that Christian children make the same mistakes that their pagan friends do? That is why it is very important that we believe the ***truth*** of God's word

The apostle Paul gives us instructions on how to overcome the devil's schemes. He starts out with an emphasis on **truth**:

*"Stand firm with the **belt of truth** buckled around your waist." Ephesians 6:14*

First of all, we must stand—not lie down and play dead. There is a saying: "If you don't stand for something, you'll fall for anything." Let's reword this saying: "If you don't stand for the truth, you'll fall for the lie." Do you know the **truth**? Do you know your Bible? How will you be able to identify the lie, if you don't know the **truth**?

Paul also tells us to take up the shield of *faith*, with which you can extinguish all the flaming arrows *(lies and deception)* of the evil one. Faith in the living word of God and His faithfulness will stop the arrows of deception before they even reach your heart. Do you have a living *faith* in God and His word? He and His word are one.

Power Principle #12
You can't trust God, if you don't believe His word.

Next, Paul tells us to take the helmet of salvation and the sword of the Spirit, which is the *word of God*. God has given us the mind of Christ, a mind that is sound and able to see things as they really are. With His word, we can demolish all *strongholds of the enemy*—we can kick the devil out of our lives and live a life that is pleasing to God.

At one time, King David and his men were forced to live with their wives and children in caves in order to escape the murderous King Saul. In the midst of his circumstances, he cried out:

"The LORD is my rock, my fortress and my deliverer; my God is my rock, in whom I take refuge, my shield and the horn of my salvation. He is my stronghold, my refuge and my savior—from violent men you save me." 2 Samuel 22:2,3

No matter what you have been through, you can choose to allow God to be your source of protection—your **stronghold**, your place of safety from the evil in this world.

Points to Ponder…

- What are your fears?
- Wonder where they came from?
- Have you ever been molested or abused physically by a loved one?
- Have you ever been abandoned, rejected or betrayed by someone you love?
- If so, have you allowed Jesus to heal your broken heart?
- Have you made a conscious decision to forgive everyone who has ever hurt you?
- Can you quote a scripture from your heart that applies to everyday life?

Quiet Time…

Dearest Heavenly Father,

Lord, I have sinned against You in thought, word, and deed. I need Your forgiveness, and the grace to forgive others who have offended me. I desire to be Your vessel of mercy, and I ask that You reveal any person whom I have failed to forgive. I don't want to hold onto anything in my past. I want to be set free of all the strongholds in my life. Lord, do a miracle in my life and set my heart free to love You perfectly with an undivided heart. I love You. I am Yours, and You are forever mine. *Amen.*

You are my hiding place;
you will protect me from trouble and surround me with songs of deliverance. Psalms 32:7

CHAPTER 7

The *Prize*

My son, if you accept my words and store up my commands within you, turning your ear to wisdom and applying your heart to understanding, and if you call out for insight and cry aloud for understanding, and if you look for it as for silver and search for it as for hidden treasure, then you will understand the fear of the LORD and find the knowledge of God. Proverbs 2:1-5

There is a process of preparation for service in the King's court, and it is a path that leads to the treasures of God's kingdom. The question is how bad do you want it? Are you willing to give up all that your heart treasures in order to do what God requires? If so, then Proverbs 2:1-5 say that you must:

- *Accept God's word* as the ultimate authority in your life. His word is the truth that will set you free from the powers of darkness and lead you on a path of righteous living.
- *Store up His commands* within your heart, for out of the abundance of the heart the mouth speaks.
- *Call out*, or desperately pray, for insight and understanding.
- *Search or seek for understanding* as if it were a chest of "hidden treasure".

If you do this, God promises that you will understand the fear of the LORD, which is the beginning of wisdom, and find the knowledge of God! God wants you to find Him; and then, He wants you to get to know Him as He really is. When you really know Him, you will fall madly in love with Him; and motivated by love, you will desire to live a life that brings glory and honor to Him. This is the secret that will unlock your future.

While speaking to a crowd of thousands, many poor among them, Jesus shocked His listeners when He told them:

"And why do you worry about clothes? See how the lilies of the field grow. They do not labor or spin. Yet I tell you that not even Solomon in all his splendor was dressed like one of these. If that is how God clothes the grass of the field, which is here today and tomorrow is thrown into the fire, will he not much more clothe you, O you of little faith? So do not worry, saying, `What shall we eat?' or `What shall we drink?' or `What shall we wear?' For the pagans run after all these things, and your heavenly Father knows that you need them. But seek first His kingdom and His righteousness, and all these things will be given to you at well." Matthew 6:28-33

Jesus could see the human heart with its cares and concerns. It is human nature to be concerned about the daily needs of survival. In our country, it is hard to imagine that we would have to worry about where our next meal is coming from, because we have an abundance of food in the grocery stores, our freezers and pantries. However, most of humanity throughout the ages has struggled to keep from starving to death! For many millions throughout the world today, clean water to drink or bathe in is an unheard-of luxury. And how many more live in cardboard shelters or on the streets of large cities. These are legitimate needs, not wants. Yet, if our heart is gripped with fear and anxiety, we are distracted from pursuing *the prize*. That is why Jesus assures us that God will provide for all of our needs, when we seek Him and His Kingdom first.

Jesus was speaking to over 5,000 people who had gathered to hear Him preach His famous sermon on the mount. Most of those gathered on that day were the poor and the downtrodden. The Roman government held them captive to poverty through high taxation, while the religious leaders put a yoke of religious rules on the back of the people. They had no hope other than the promised Messiah.

In His sermon, Jesus told the people not to worry about their physical needs for food, clothing and shelter. He promised that, if they sought first the kingdom of God and

His righteousness, He would meet all of these needs, in addition to meeting their spiritual needs. You see, we are so easily distracted from the *prize* that is set before us.

We spend many of our days like Don Quixote— chasing windmills.

For those of us who are not starving or living on the streets, it is even harder to find the treasures of His Kingdom! We are busy seeking beautifully wrapped counterfeits for the heavenly treasures: **POSITION, POSSESSIONS, POWER, POPULARITY, PLEASURE, PRESTIGE**, and other idols of our society! Jesus told His disciples:

"I tell you the truth, it is hard for a rich man to enter the kingdom of heaven. Again, I tell you, it is easier for a camel to go through the eye of a needle than for a rich man to enter the kingdom of God." When the disciples heard this, they were greatly astonished and asked, "Who then can be saved?" Matthew 19:23-25

The disciples were blown away by His comment. After all, the religious leaders and the rulers of the Sanhedrin were not hurt for money. Did Jesus mean even they would have a hard time entering the kingdom of heaven? The Pharisees followed the letter of the Law of Moses, yet did their religious perfection not qualify them for the Kingdom? Thank God, Jesus didn't forget about us! He looked at them and said,

"With man this is impossible, but with God all things are possible."
Matthew 19:26

For a rich man—and anyone who lives in the United States of America is rich by the world's standards—the distractions of idolatry are not the only weapons Satan uses to take us down the wrong path. Our hearts can be clouded with anxiety, fear, doubt, bitterness, greed, and other cares of this world that choke out the Word of God! Our vision and focus remain earthbound!

> **Power Principle #13**
> *You will never find heavenly treasures, while you are giving God your backside!*

God's word commands us to seek Him!

"When I shut up the heavens so that there is no rain, or command locusts to devour the land or send a plague among my people, if my people, who are called by my name, will humble themselves and pray and seek my face and turn from their wicked ways, then will I hear from heaven and will forgive their sin and will heal their land." 2 Chronicles 7:13,14

When we are busy doing our "own thing"—taking care of our own plans, purposes, and agendas—we are walking in wicked ways. Rather than waiting for our orders from Jesus, our Commander in Chief, we are AWOL *(absent without leave)*—busy building our own kingdoms. Our neighbors see church goers who basically live their lives the same ways they do—running here, running there, building this, building that —no time to reach out to the lonely, the widows, the orphans, or the aliens in their distress.

Many in the church today are living their lives for ***their own pleasure***, while God's word tells us that we were created ***for His pleasure***. This is evil, and we must turn from our wicked ways and seek the face of God. Our nation depends upon it! God is calling us to repent of our own ways to serve Him.

Gather together, gather together, O shameful nation, before the appointed time arrives and that day sweeps on like chaff, before the fierce anger of the LORD comes upon you, before the day of the LORD's wrath comes upon you. Seek the LORD, all you humble of the land, you who do what he commands. Seek righteousness, seek humility; perhaps you will be sheltered on the day of the LORD's anger. Zephaniah 2:1-3

God is calling born again believers, those who have humbled themselves and who obey His commands, to seek the LORD—seek righteousness and humility. Isn't this contrary to what the world teaches us? We are told by our culture to demand our rights, even at the expense of others. We want it our way, and we want it now. Among those who fill our churches are thieves who legally steal from others in the name of malpractice and/or liability. Some Christians vote for evil men who will not defend the lives of unborn children. Some pastors justify ridiculous salaries and housing allowances, while single mothers in the church struggle financially to keep a roof over the heads of their children. I could go on—yes, people of God—we need to repent of our evil ways and seek the face of God. It may not be too late.

Why does God tell us to seek ***humility***?

Webster says...

Humility:
1. *a state of being humble;*
2. *not proud or haughty;*
3. *not arrogant or assertive;*
4. *insignificant;*
5. *not pretentious;*
6. *to destroy power, independence, or prestige of*

God's heart is close to the humble—those who acknowledge their own depravity and need of Him. His word tells us:

"Has not my hand made all these things, and so they came into being?" declares the LORD. "This is the one I esteem: he who is humble and contrite in spirit, and trembles at my word." Isaiah 66:2

God's word tells us that He esteems a **humble** person. Wow! Imagine that. If you want to impress God, you must be humble—oh, and also contrite in spirit. In other words, you must be really miserable over your own sins.

I had just gone through a painful divorce and lost custody of my precious little boy, Rocky. Although I had everything the world said that would make me happy, I was miserable and suicidal. Oh, I had it all: a college education, a great job, travel to exotic places, the man of my dreams, fancy cars, jewelry, and clothes. Yet, I was miserable and wanted to die. I once was an independent spirit, in need of no one—and now, I was a broken young woman. God's word tells us to:

Submit yourselves, then, to God. Resist the devil, and he will flee from you. Come near to God and he will come near to you. Wash your hands, you sinners, and purify your hearts, you double-minded. Grieve, mourn and wail. Change your laughter to mourning and your joy to gloom. Humble yourselves before the Lord, and He will lift you up. James 4:7-10

God allowed me to fall all the way to the bottom of the pit, so that I could look up. There wasn't anywhere else I could find healing for my broken heart. God's word tells us to:

Seek the LORD while He may be found; call on Him while He is near. Let the wicked forsake his way and the evil man his thoughts. Let him turn to the LORD, and he will have mercy on him, and to our God, for he will freely pardon. Isaiah 55:6,7

You know, it really isn't a suggestion for those who call themselves Christians. Why must God continually cry out to us from His word? It is because we are stubborn and rebellious people.

Power Principle #13
You will never find heavenly treasures, while you are giving God your backside!

I was such a person. Yes, I had been a church member all my life. I even had a hunger for more of God and a desire to please Him. When I heard the message of salvation in an Episcopal church, I rejoiced and eagerly said the sinner's prayer. I confessed that I was a sinner and asked Jesus to come into my heart. However, no one ever told me that I had to make Him Lord of my life, and that I would have to obey His word. I call that a cheap gospel—the kind that is taught in many churches. The result was disastrous—my marriage ended in divorce, and I lost custody of my precious son, and found myself far from the purposes of God.

Thank God for His unending mercies and unconditional love. After two years of a living hell, I looked up and saw the face of God. He forgave my sins and restored my soul. That glorious day, the love of God gave me hope and a purpose to live. Little did I know that He would take me from trials to triumph and that I would live to tell about it.

If we are to fulfill God's divine purpose for our lives, we must prepare our hearts for His kingdom. The prophet Hosea commands us to:

Sow for yourselves righteousness, reap the fruit of unfailing love, and break up your unplowed ground; for it is time to seek the LORD, until he comes and showers righteousness on you. Hosea 10:12

Do not be deceived: God cannot be mocked. A man reaps what he sows. The one who sows to please his sinful nature, from that nature will reap destruction; the one who sows to please the Spirit, from the Spirit will reap eternal life. Let us not become weary in doing good, for at the proper time we will reap a harvest if we do not give up. Galatians 6:7-9

We have a promise from God: if we sow righteousness in our lives, we will reap the fruit of unfailing love. Isn't that what you are looking for? Well, it won't be found in the arms of a man, or in the applause of an audience. It won't be found in a fat bank account or a fulfilled career or a house full of children. It can only be found in a childlike relationship with the God of love. God's word tells us that:

*Blessed are they whose ways are blameless, who walk according to the law of the LORD. Blessed are they who keep his statutes and **seek him** with all their heart. They do nothing wrong; they walk in his ways. Psalms 119:1-3*

My life took a radical turn in 1980, when I made Jesus the Lord of my life. No longer was He just my savior—He was now the ultimate authority in my life. His Word told me to love my enemies, so I did. He told me to forgive everyone for every offense, so I did. He told me to tithe, so I did. He hates divorce, so I do, too. He is concerned about the widows, fatherless children, and aliens in their distress, so I am, too. He hates pornography and abortion, so I do, too. He is merciful, so I am, also. I could go on, but you get the picture.

This kind of love relationship with God did not take root in my life until I decided to love God more than myself. I had to be willing to put my own happiness on the back burner in order to please God. This is what it means to take up your cross daily and follow Jesus. The cross is the place of worship, whereby we put to death all that we desire in order to do what is right in God's sight. When we seek first the kingdom of God and His righteousness, we find intimacy with the Creator of the universe.

What an awesome privilege we have been given. The sad truth is that many Christians sitting in pews in America's churches today will miss this incredible blessing and never fulfill God's potential in their lives. Are you one of them? You don't have to be.

God's mercies are new every morning—just waiting for you to respond to His call.

The writer of Hebrews tells us that:

By faith Enoch was taken from this life, so that he did not experience death; he could not be found, because God had taken him away. For before he was taken, he was commended as one who pleased God. And without faith it is impossible to please God, because anyone who comes to Him must believe that He exists and that He rewards those who earnestly seek Him. Hebrews 11:5,6

By faith, Enoch was commended by God as one who pleased Him. Awesome! He was rewarded for his faithfulness and walked right into heaven, never tasting death. Isn't that what most Christians are hoping for in the near future? Churches are full of people who are counting on the rapture so that they will not taste death, nor face the realities of the Tribulation period.

However, we need to get a reality check! This reward is set apart for those who, by faith, earnestly **seek Him**. This promise is not for pew-sitting worldly-minded carnal Christians. Now, I hope this doesn't upset your doctrinal applecart, because your doctrine won't get you to heaven.

Power Principle #14
*God is pleased with people who **run to Him** by faith, walk **with Him** by faith, and **live for Him** through faith.*

How can you have this kind of faith-driven life? The recipe is simple, and the ingredients are few. Mix together a sacrificial life with an intimate relationship with God the Father, through Jesus the Son. Anoint with the oil of the Holy Spirit and put into the oven of affliction. At the appointed time, pour out to a dead and dying world.

King Hezekiah was one of the few kings of Judah who did what was right in God's eyes. Centuries after his death, we are still able to read about this great man of God:

This is what Hezekiah did throughout Judah, doing what was good and right and faithful before the LORD his God. In everything that he undertook in the service of God's temple and in obedience to the law and the commands, he sought his God and worked wholeheartedly, and so he prospered. 2 Chronicles 31:20,21

Can you imagine how wonderful it would be if someone was able to write your epitaph like that? Just imagine: Here lies Connie Cenac, a handmaiden in the King's court. In everything she did in service to the Lord and in obedience to God's royal law of love, she sought Her God and worked wholeheartedly, and so she prospered! If I go first, will someone please have this engraved on my tombstone?

Everybody talks about prosperity. Many people think that if the right man gets elected, we will prosper. If the stock market rises in value, we will prosper. If my 401K increases in value, I will prosper. If I win the lottery, I will prosper. These are all wrong presumptions. According to God's word, prosperity is a blessing that comes when we seek the Lord and then put feet to our prayers. We must simply get in the game and work hard.

The Bible says that God prospers the hands of the diligent—not the lazy. He says that, if we are faithful with the little that He gives us, He will entrust us with more. Today, churches in America are full of Christians who are still seeking after the wealth of this world. They store up wealth for their old age, rather than share with the poor. They play the stock market, and gamble with the lottery. They steal from their employers and file lawsuits whenever the opportunity arises, all with the hopes of getting rich. God's word tells us just how wrong we are. He says:

I love those who love me, and those who seek me find me. With me are riches and honor, enduring wealth and prosperity. Proverbs 8:17,18

God says that He loves those who love Him. That is why Jesus said that you can't serve both God and money. He is a jealous God, and He will not tolerate spiritual adultery—that is idolatry. You cannot serve both God and your financial goals. He is looking for men and women who are single-minded—who will serve Him faithfully, wholeheartedly, and sacrificially.

He promises that if you seek Him, you will find Him—and then, guess what comes with the package—riches and honor, enduring wealth and prosperity. Does that mean that we will all be flying our private jets to our villas on the Riviera? No, of course not. But it does mean that all of our legitimate needs will be met— and then some. Listen to this promise:

Delight yourself in the LORD and he will give you the desires of your heart. Psalms 37:4

What do you delight in? Who makes your heart sing? Turn your heart to Jesus, the lover of your soul, and prosper!

Points to Ponder...

- What do you desire more than anything in this world?
- Do you seek the approval of men over the approval of God?
- Are you storing up wealth? Are you stingy with others?
- Do you have concern for the poor in your own church?
- Are you compassionate towards the poor and hungry in the world?
- Are you faithful? Do you honor your word, even when it hurts?
- Are you trustworthy? Can God trust you with His wealth?
- Would you rather be in a crowd or alone with God?

Quiet Time...

Dearest Heavenly Father,

Lord, I confess that I am easily distracted by the glitz and glitter of this world, while I should be seeking a deeper relationship with You. I have also allowed the cares of this world to cloud my vision of who You are. Please forgive me for being double minded. Cleanse my heart, oh Lord, and deliver me from the love of this world, that I might seek You with all of my heart, with all of my soul, and with all of my mind. I love You. I am Yours, and You are forever mine. *Amen.*

O God, you are my God, earnestly I seek you; my soul thirsts for you, my body longs for you, in a dry and weary land where there is no water.
Psalms 63:1

CHAPTER 8

The Fear of the *LORD*

The fear of the LORD is the beginning of wisdom; all who follow his precepts have good understanding. Psalms 111.10

I magine that you have just come into a vast inheritance of wealth. In addition to the millions of tax-free dollars that are sitting in the estate, you have been given foresight and wisdom to use the money in a way that will bring eternal blessings to many. You have also been given divine knowledge, and a treasure chest filled with unconditional love, unspeakable joy, peace of mind, patience, understanding, and other riches too numerous to mention.

Imagine that you never bother to go to see the executor of the estate to collect your inheritance. The money sits in a non-interest-bearing account while you struggle to pay your bills on your measly salary. You are so busy working overtime in order to make ends meet, you never take a vacation or get a day off on the weekend. You are so busy trying to do it all on your own, you never realize that a treasure chest is waiting for you to be opened filled with treasures that will give you all your heart desires, treasures that will equip you to fulfill your divine destiny.

Well, this is exactly how most Christians live. You don't have to, you know. Your inheritance is waiting for you to claim. Jesus said:

"Ask and it will be given to you; seek and you will find; knock and the door will be opened to you. For everyone who asks receives; he who seeks finds; and to him who knocks, the door will be opened." Matthew 7:7,8

We know that all of the blessings of our eternal inheritance are "hidden" in Jesus Christ and that He is our treasure chest! However, you know that any treasure chest worth its weight in gold is kept locked until the proper owner comes to retrieve it. How then do we unlock the secret treasures that are hidden in Christ? The prophet Isaiah tells us that:

The LORD is exalted, for he dwells on high; he will fill Zion with justice and righteousness. He will be the sure foundation for your times, a rich store of salvation and wisdom and knowledge; the fear of the LORD is the key to this treasure. Isaiah 33:5,6

If the key to the treasures of God's kingdom is the *fear of the LORD*, then we need a clear understanding of this verse. I really believe that we have, for the most part, been given a cheap version of the gospel in America. Many in churches today really believe that, because they walked the aisle, said a sinner's prayer and got baptized, they now have the liberty to go on with life as usual. This is the main reason why most Christians will never fulfill their divine purpose in life.

I came to understand the meaning of this verse when I realized that, by living my life according to the standards of this world, I brought pain and suffering to myself and to those I loved. I began to see that God requires obedience, and He disciplines those whom He loves. The *fear of the LORD* is a beautiful thing!

You know, it is natural to want a good education. College education is a key to getting a good job, it opens doors of opportunity that are closed to those without the proper credentials. However, what happens with all of that knowledge if you do not have wisdom? Wisdom enables a person to use the knowledge that they have in a prudent fashion.

For example, most people who win the lottery are bankrupt within five years. Why? It is because they lack wisdom. Many professional athletes, who make millions of dollars in their early years, are bankrupt within a few years of retirement for the same reason. And what about the movie stars and celebrities: though they earn millions of dollars each year, most cannot seem to have a happy marriage. They go from one broken relationship to another, many times covering the pain of a broken heart with alcohol or drugs. Why? It is because they lack wisdom.

My husband, Dwight, became a C.P.A. *(Certified Public Accountant)* and was brilliant in accounting; however, for a time prior to coming to Christ, he had a serious gambling problem. His education and training in financial matters were worthless, because he could not hold on to the money that he earned.

Power Principle #15
Knowledge without wisdom is worthless.

God tells us that the ***fear of the LORD*** is the beginning of wisdom. You cannot begin to make right choices in life until you have discovered the fear of the LORD. Wisdom comes from the mind of Christ—which is given to those who sit under the shadow of His wing to learn from Him. Wisdom leads to all other treasures found in the heart of God. Wisdom prepares you for service in the King's court. That is why God's word commands us to:

Fear the LORD your God, serve him only and take your oaths in his name. Do not follow other gods, the gods of the peoples around you; for the LORD your God, who is among you, is a jealous God and his anger will burn against you, and he will destroy you from the face of the land. Deuteronomy 6:13-15

We are all tempted to worship the gods of our culture—yes, even we Christians are tempted to live our lives in the pursuit of pleasure, power, possessions, prestige, and popularity. Aren't those the idols of our century? That is why we are called to turn from these wicked ways and pursue the kingdom of God and His righteousness.

"I tell you, my friends, do not be afraid of those who kill the body and after that can do no more. But I will show you whom you should fear: fear Him who, after killing of the body, has power to throw you into Hell. Yes, I tell you, fear Him." Luke 12:4,5

Now surely, our loving Savior wouldn't say anything so harsh! It cannot possibly mean what it sounds like, could it? Well, I looked up the definition of fear in the dictionary, and you will not believe what it means.

Webster says...

Fear:
  1. An unpleasant, often strong emotion caused by anticipation or awareness of danger;
  *2. A profound reverence and **awe**, especially towards God*

Do you know that the word ***awe*** means to ***tremble with dread?*** That is real fear. I wonder why we don't hear more of this from the pulpit? Are preachers afraid to run off the sheep?

In some ways, a cheap Gospel has led many down the wide road that leads to destruction. In our attempts to "lure" the sinner to the cross and ultimate salvation, we have presented God as the all-merciful, forgiving God that He is, without first telling of His Holiness, His hatred of sin, and His coming wrath. As a result, many have made confessions of faith, been water-baptized, sing in the choir, and teach Sunday school—all the while, they remain sinners headed for Hell. The Bible tells us about Uzziah, a young king of Judah who did what was right in the eyes of the Lord, unlike most of the kings who had preceded him.

*He sought God during the days of Zechariah, who instructed him in **the fear of God**. As long as he sought the LORD, God gave him success. 2 Chronicles 26:5*

Now, isn't that what everyone in the whole world wants? Success! People want to be successful in business, in family life, in marriage—people just want to succeed. People go to college, buy self-help books, go to seminars, and chase the wind trying to find a quick fix recipe that will help them to succeed. Well, God already wrote a best seller—the Bible is the best self-help book you could ever read. And He has given us the recipe for success: Uzziah was instructed in the *fear of the LORD* and was successful as long as he sought the LORD. You see, the two ingredients go hand in hand—like peanut butter and jelly.

Power Principle #16
The fear of the LORD helps us to recognize our need for God's mercy and forgiveness, drawing us to seek His face.

When I found myself in the pit of despair after doing things my way, I finally understood the *fear of the LORD* and ran back to Him. That is why the Bible says:

The LORD delights in those who fear Him, who put their hope in his unfailing love. Psalms 147:11

The apostle Paul reminded the church at Corinth that:

We must all appear before the judgment seat of Christ, that each one may receive what is due him for the things done while in the body, whether good or bad.
Since, then, we know what it is to fear the LORD, we try to persuade men. 2 Corinthians 5:10,11

Paul says that there is a day coming when every person who ever lived will stand before the judgment seat of Christ. On this day of reckoning, each of us will receive what is due to us for the things we did while on this earth—the good, the bad, and the ugly. Now, I don't know about you, but I really do not want my dirty laundry hung out to dry in front of the whole universe. That is why I search my heart daily, and in every way possible, repent of any evil that may be lurking in the crevices of my heart. Like Paul, I know what it is to fear the LORD, and that is why I spend my valuable time trying to persuade men and women to fear the LORD.

What you know in your heart to be true really does motivate you to do what you do. The important thing is to know the truth that will set you free from the deception of this world. There was a time when I thought I knew God. I had said the sinner's prayer, been water baptized, and went to church every Sunday. One day, because I did not know the *fear of the LORD*, I chose to disobey God's command, got a divorce and entered into a sinful relationship with Dwight. My backsliding did not end until I had lost everything of real value. I am not the only one who has missed the mark. We have all sinned and fallen short of the glory of God. That is why we need a Savior.

We have heard all about the love of God, and surely, God is love. However, God is also holy and just. Because sin is actually a rebellion against His rule on the earth, it must be punished. That is why He sent Jesus to take the punishment for our sins. There is a time to have a fear based upon the wrath of an all-powerful, Almighty God. Sinners and saints alike are told to take heed. That awesome and terrible Day of the LORD will come. That is why the apostle Paul warns us:

Therefore, my dear friends, as you have always obeyed--not only in my presence, but now much more in my absence—continue to work out your salvation with fear and trembling, for it is God who works in you to will and to act according to his good purpose. Philippians 2:12,13

Why does Paul say that we must continue to work out our salvation with fear and trembling? He's talking about the *fear of the Lord*. We need to understand that our walk with God is a day-to-day experience of laying down our own plans and agendas in order to do the will of the Father. Thank God it is He who gives us the will to act according to His good purpose.

A wise man understands that a day is coming when God will punish all sinners who have not taken refuge under the blood of Jesus. That is why we are commanded to:

Serve the LORD with fear and rejoice with trembling. Kiss the Son, lest he be angry and you be destroyed in your way, for his wrath can flare up in a moment. Blessed are all who take refuge in him. Psalms 2:11,12

Doesn't this psalm sound like an oxymoron? How does a person serve with fear, yet rejoice with trembling? It does not make sense on the surface. However, if we listen to the many parables told by Jesus concerning the wise and faithful servant vs. the unfaithful servant, we can get a clue.

The employees who work in our company understand that if they do not fulfill their job responsibilities as required, they can lose their job. It does not matter that Dwight, and I love our employees and want to bless them. We cannot bless an unfaithful employee. If an employee comes to work late every day, or gets drunk on the job, we will be forced to discipline the guilty party. However, 99% of our employees do a great job, not out of fear of getting fired, but because they are faithful and diligent in character. Most of them really enjoy their work and minister to one another in the work place. This is how we are told to serve God. When we do, we are able to draw close enough to Jesus that we can kiss Him. He promises to bless all who take refuge in him, including you.

Power Principle #17
The fear of the LORD leads to an intimate knowledge of God.

Throughout the Old Testament, God revealed His awesome character: His love, holiness, faithfulness, mercy and judgment are revealed by His awesome deeds. He gave Himself to the children of Israel; and by His Word and His deeds, they could **know Him**. God made Himself known—Who He is, what He is like—so that we could understand the *fear of the LORD* and find life!

When the Israelites crossed the Jordan River on dry land, they set up a memorial with twelve stones. It was such a miraculous event, that Joshua wanted it to be a reminder of what God had done for His people. This is what he told the people:

"For the LORD your God dried up the Jordan before you until you had crossed over. The LORD your God did to the Jordan just what he had done to the Red Sea when he dried it up before us until we had crossed over. He did this so that all the peoples of the earth might know that the hand of the LORD is powerful and so that you might always fear the LORD your God." Joshua 4:23,24

If I had really understood how holy God is, and how He views sin, I would have never made the choices that broke my heart and devastated my life. Knowing God like I do today, I would never want to offend Him by sinning willfully. God wants us to know Him as He really is—not as our culture has made Him out to be. That is why He gave us the written word—it reveals His character. It is also why He sent Jesus —because if you get to know Jesus, you will know the Father.

Power Principle #18
A wise man sees danger and seeks refuge.

The first step towards safety is to know that danger exists. If the captain of the Titanic had known the danger that lurked in the unseen waters of the dark North Atlantic, he would have changed the course of the ship and saved the lives of his passengers and crew. The Hall of Faith found in the book of Hebrews tells us about another ship captain who built his vessel—one designed by God:

By faith Noah, when warned about things not yet seen, in holy fear built an ark to save his family. By his faith he condemned the world and became heir of the righteousness that comes by faith. Hebrews 11:7

God wants the world to know that He is a righteous judge who must punish sin. However, the world system has convinced the majority of the Americans that:

- there is no such thing as sin;
- if there is a God, He was portrayed by a cigar-smoking George Burns in the movie, *"O God"*;
- if God really does exist, He is all-loving, and would never punish someone who has never robbed a bank or committed murder by sending them to Hell;
- Hell is a place usually mentioned in attorney jokes;
- Hell is not a real place—and if it is, it was prepared for Hitler and the likes.

Thus, the sinner, seeking after the riches of this world, going about his business blinded to the truth of his peril, has no fear of God. What about you? God has called you to be His mouthpiece, as well as His vessel of mercy to those who are perishing. Are you willing?

Power Principle #19
A wise person is aware of his own sins and character flaws.

Most people, including those who attend church, rarely see their own sin. Oh, other people see it, especially family members and people who work together; but, rarely do we see our own shortcomings. We also tend to believe that, if we don't smoke, chew tobacco, drink alcohol, chase women, or play the slot machines, we are good Christians—God is pleased with us. However, God's word gives us a description of a wicked person. It says:

An oracle is within my heart concerning the sinfulness of the wicked: there is no fear of God before his eyes. For in his own eyes he flatters himself too much to detect or hate his sin. The words of his mouth are wicked and deceitful; he has ceased to be wise and to do good. Even on his bed he plots evil; he commits himself to a sinful course and does not reject what is wrong. Psalms 36:1-4

Unfortunately, too many Christians fit this description. First, there is no fear of God before her eyes. Instead, in her own eyes, she flatters herself and does not detect or hate her own sin. In most cases, she is busy finding fault with others and gossiping about them. Her words are wicked and deceitful. She will even lie against an employer in order to get workers' compensation or some other false claim. She will stir up dissension in the workplace or at church. She will berate her husband, because he is just not spiritual enough. She will squander her time and money on selfish desires. She will sleep with a man she is not married to. She commits herself to a sinful course rather than turning back to God and His ways. She does not reject what is evil in God's eyes.

It is unfortunate that India's leader Ghandi once said, "I would become a Christian, if I ever met one." The people who know you best are the people you live with and those that you work with. Is there enough evidence in your life to convict you of being a Christian, if it were against the law?

Power Principle #20
The fear of the LORD leads to life.

The fear of the LORD leads to life: Then one rests content, untouched by trouble.
Proverbs 19:23

Can you imagine a life of contentment, untouched by trouble? Most people think this is accomplished by accumulating enough wealth so that they can retire and go fishing or golfing the rest of their lives. As long as there is money in the bank, everything will go smoothly, and stress will just fade away. This is the great lie of our century. We all know that money cannot buy happiness. All you have to do is look at the wealthy celebrities who cannot seem to find contentment with the wife of their youth. It also won't buy good health or save a child from cancer or make people love you. According to God's word, there is only one way to find peace and contentment. It begins with the *fear of the LORD*.

Life is full of problems, and no one is exempt. Bad things do happen to good people, because we live in a fallen world. However, for the person who has discovered the *fear of the Lord*, there is hope. Wonder why? Well, it is because the person who fears God will choose to obey Him, and obedience brings blessing.

Dwight and I have been falsely accused of fraud, faced a grand jury investigation, sued by a visitor in our home, sued at work by employees who accused us of everything under the sun, rejected and betrayed by people we loved, called cult leaders and control freaks by other Christians, rejected by Dwight's family, and embezzled by family and friends, just to name a few. Because we chose to forgive and love our enemies, we have been blessed beyond measure. *God is awesome!*

Power Principle #21
The fear of the LORD leads to a long and fruitful to life.

The fear of the LORD adds length to life, but the years of the wicked are cut short. Proverbs 10:27

It really makes sense, when you think about it. Those who ignore God and His ways generally live very unhealthy lives. First of all, sexual immorality is usually the first step towards death. It leads to all types of sicknesses, and many are fatal. In addition, sex sin leads to demonic activity, which brings about a sickness of the soul called guilt. In order to hide the guilt, many are led into captivity to alcohol and/or illegal drugs. Mind-altering drugs lead into further demonic activity, called a depraved mind. At this point, a person with a depraved mind cannot even consider making healthy life choices.

Consider the pregnant woman, who adds fuel to the fire by choosing to abort and kill her unborn child. The very act of abortion can lead to the physical death of the mother; and certainly, it leaves an emptiness of soul that only Jesus can fill. Murder is sin, and it causes the woman's heart to be hardened even further so that love cannot penetrate. Many women who abort their babies become sterile or cannot carry another baby to term. What a loss—the right to an abortion replaces the ability to bring forth life.

Add to this list of death producing behaviors, and we see that our nation has become a land of gluttons who kill themselves with every bite of processed food. Yes, truly, the wage of sin is death.

Thank God for His mercies that are new every morning. No matter how badly we've messed up, we can live a long life as a servant in the King's court. Our lives will bring glory to God, when we discover *the fear of the LORD*.

Power Principle #22
The fear of the LORD is like a steering wheel on a vehicle.
It is used to turn us away from the snares of death.

The fear of the LORD is a fountain of life, turning a man from the snares of death.
Proverbs 14:27

When a baby is born into this fallen world, he is destined for death. It is our human nature—the fallen nature that is in rebellion towards God. Left to our own devices, we will kill, steal and destroy. We will trample on other people in order to please ourselves. We will break every commandment of God and won't feel a bit sorry for it. It is hard to believe that every little baby in the hospital nursery, barely out of the womb, has the nature of death.

God has given us the antibiotic that will kill the disease of death. Because God is the source of life, He came to Earth and bore our sins and our death on the cross of Jesus Christ—and then, He rose from the dead, defeating death and the grave, to give us eternal life. If you have discovered the fear of the LORD and have surrendered your will to the Lord Jesus Christ, then you already have eternal life. When your mortal body ceases to live, you will go from glory to glory and step into eternity with the Giver of Life.

Have you taken hold of the fear of the LORD? Does your life tell the story of this great redemption? Can you honestly say, "I once was lost, but now I'm saved, was blind, but now I see!"

Power Principle #23
We must instill the fear of the LORD in our children.

The sad truth is that many Christian parents have failed to teach their children about the fear of the LORD. As a result, too many young people in American churches get caught up in the same web of sin that their public school peers get into.

Come, my children, listen to me; I will teach you the fear of the LORD. Whoever of you loves life and desires to see many good days, keep your tongue from evil and your lips from speaking lies. Psalms 34:11-13

If we want to raise children that can be trusted to make choices that are pleasing to God, then we must teach them to fear God. The fear of the LORD will keep a person from evil speech and deception.

When we were raising our children, we were very honest with them about our own mistakes in life. We not only told them what we did wrong, we also told them about the suffering we caused to others. We asked the older children who were affected by the divorce to forgive us, and we made a commitment to stay married to each other until death. And then, we did our best to instill the fear of the LORD into their hearts. In spite of our mistakes, all of our children are awesome people. Our daughters are wonderful Christian wives and mothers who are raising their children in the fear of the LORD. The curse has been broken over our children! *Hallelujah!*

Jesus, who is our example, is described as:

A shoot will come up from the stump of Jesse; from his roots a Branch will bear fruit. The Spirit of the LORD will rest on him--the Spirit of wisdom and of understanding, the Spirit of counsel and of power, the spirit of knowledge and of the fear of the LORD— and he will delight in the fear of the LORD. Isaiah 11:1-3 Jesus delighted in the fear of the LORD. Can you imagine that the One Who spoke the worlds into existence gets a thrill from the fear of the LORD? There is good reason for this:

Who, then, is the man that fears the LORD? He will spend his days in prosperity, and his descendants will inherit the land. The LORD confides in those who fear Him; He makes His covenant known to them. Psalms 25:12-14

Now, that is a mouthful. What a bundle of promises! First of all, the one who fears the LORD will spend her days in prosperity. There you go again—everyone wants to prosper, but true prosperity is the reward for those who fear of the LORD.

Even better than that—God promises to confide in those who fear Him. I know a lot of people, but I only confide in my very best friends—those who love me and can be trusted with my secrets. And that is just how God is with us. He knows those who can be trusted with the secrets of His kingdom, and He delights to reveal His plans to those who love and fear Him. It is really great to be best friends with God. You ought to try it.

Power Principle #24
The fear of the LORD, when combined with humility, brings wealth and honor and life.

Humility and the fear of the LORD bring wealth and honor and life. Proverbs 22:4

If I did an infomercial on television and guaranteed that my formula for success was foolproof—and that it was absolutely free—do you think people would be setting aside all of their own agendas to get my recipe for success? I think so. Well, the recipe for wealth, honor, and life has two ingredients: humility and the fear of the LORD. How hard is that? Why don't we hear more of this in the pulpit? Forget the name it and claim it gospel—we've got the real thing, here.

We have already talked about humility, but I'll give you a very brief description of humility. It simply means that you see yourself through God's eyes. We are not God —He is. We are like dumb sheep. Sheep are the dumbest animals on the face of the earth. Without a shepherd, they will eat bad food and die of thirst. They literally do not have enough sense to get out of the rain—and they will leave a perfectly good pasture and wander off, where they will be eaten by lions, and tigers, and bears! Oh, my! Now that you have discovered the truth about yourself, just get some fear of the LORD, and you are on your way to victory!

Why wait for another big mistake—take hold of the mighty and merciful hand of God and let Him lead you to green pastures.

Power Principle #25
God's love and compassion is for those who fear Him.

There is a wonderful song that says, "As high as the heavens are above the earth, so great is the father's love—as far as the east is from the west, so far has He taken our sin from us!" I love that song, but it is not exactly accurate. You see, this promise is actually found in the Psalms, and it really says:

For as high as the heavens are above the earth, so great is His love for those who fear Him; as far as the east is from the west, so far has he removed our transgressions from us. As a father has compassion on his children, so the LORD has compassion on those who fear Him. Psalms 103:11-13

As a compassionate father, God looks over the affairs of His children who fear Him. Very few people have grown up with compassionate fathers, and many have no clue what it means to even have a father. In addition, too many children have grown up in a home with a harsh, abusive father, or one that has gone most of the time doing his own thing. Does that describe you? If it does, this is great news! You now have a father who is not abusive or so far away that you cannot run to him when you are hurt or in a crisis. Your heavenly Father is close by, and He promises that if you draw near Him, He will draw near to you. He will pick you up when you fall down and comfort you when you are sad or hurt. After He has healed your broken heart, He will guide you down the path of life that He has chosen for you. What an awesome promise for those who fear the LORD!

Have you put your hope in God's unfailing love? All other loves will fail—they will bring disappointment and sorrow, but the love of God will never leave you nor forsake you. The Bible has great news for those who fear the LORD:

The angel of the LORD encamps those who fear him, and he delivers them. Taste and see that the LORD is good; blessed is the man who takes refuge in him. Fear the LORD, you his saints, for those who fear him lack nothing. Psalms 34:7-9

Points to Ponder...

- Who or what do you love more than God?
- Would you be willing to disobey God in order to please someone else?
- Are you afraid to sin against God? If not, why?
- Would you be willing to try to talk a friend out of getting an abortion?
- Would you be willing to try to talk a friend out of getting a divorce?
- Do you believe that God will discipline you if you sin?
- Do you believe that God will reward you for your obedience?

Quiet Time...

Dearest Heavenly Father,

Thank You for Your love and mercies that are new for me today and every day. I confess that I have many times wandered from Your love and followed after the things of this world. I have spent my time and resources on things that will not last—things that do not glorify Your holy name. I desperately need to know the fear of the LORD, so that I can choose to obey Your royal law of love. Help me to let go of the things that have captured my heart, so that I may seek Your face and find the love that is eternal. I love You. I am Yours, and You are forever mine. *Amen.*

Let all the earth fear the LORD; let all the people of the world revere him.
Psalms 33:8

CHAPTER 9

The *Obedient Heart*

Blessed are all who fear the LORD, who walk in his ways. You will eat the fruit of your labor; blessings and prosperity will be yours. Your wife will be like a fruitful vine within your house; your sons will be like olive shoots around your table. Thus is the man blessed who fears the LORD. Psalms 128:1-4

The person who fears the LORD is blessed, because obedience brings forth God's blessing. Everyone wants to be blessed by God. We often pray and ask God to bless our lives, our business endeavors, our nation, our family, and our friends. But the truth of the matter is that God's blessing is the fruit of an obedient life. Those who fear the Lord will walk in His ways and reap a harvest of blessing. That's a promise!

Do you remember the little guy in the comics who walked around with a rain cloud over his head all day long? Everywhere he went, that rain cloud followed him. Do you know people like that? It seems that every day is a bad hair day. Nothing goes right, ever! Well, the person who fears the Lord can have bad hair days, too; the difference is that God causes all the bad stuff to turn for good because they love God and are about the Father's business. Even the bad stuff in their lives turns into blessings. *Awesome!*

You can be a success, too. God is not a respecter of persons, and He loves you just as much as He loves me.

Power Principle #26
God will rewrite your future,
when you seek and find the fear of the LORD.

Do not be wise in your own eyes; fear the LORD and shun evil. This will bring health to your body and nourishment to your bones. Proverbs 3:7,8

Many Christians make terrible mistakes, because they foolishly think they can make wise decisions apart from the counsel of God. During our early walk with God, Dwight and I continually lost money in business because we were plain gullible. Someone would come to us with a good idea, and without seeking the counsel of God, we would jump into the new venture with both feet. We always came out on the short end of the stick.

That is why this proverb warns us not to be wise in our own eyes. There is no wisdom apart from the fear of the LORD. Today, we still have business ventures brought to us by well-meaning Christians, and we have learned to say "no". The fear of the LORD continues to help us to avoid bad decisions.

The fact of the matter is, when we make a decision to do something that God does not want us to do, it is evil. We cannot be doing our own thing and God's thing at the same time. Now, if I belong to Jesus, then I need to make sure that I am spending my time and money doing what He wants me to do—not what I want to do. Anything short of a total commitment and service to Him is sin. Job, a man who proved his commitment to God through incredible trials, said:

The fear of the Lord—that is wisdom, and to shun evil is understanding. Job 28:28

Power Principle #27
The fear of the LORD motivates us to do good and to avoid evil.

Through love and faithfulness sin is atoned for, through the fear of the LORD a man avoids evil. Proverbs 16:6

Evil is an interesting word. We sometimes think that, if we do not drink, smoke, cuss, gamble or sleep around, we are not evildoers. This fallacy has kept many Christians in a state of uselessness. It is not enough that we don't do bad things— we need to be doing the good things—and that happens to be whatever God wants us to be doing at the time.

Let's start with the basics. Go get a red-letter Bible, one that prints all of the words of Jesus in red. Then, spend some quality time reading just the red letters. Spend some time studying His sermon on the mount, where, for instance, He tells us that we must turn the other cheek, lend to others without expecting repayment, forgive everyone who ever hurt us, and love our enemies. Tough stuff. Somewhere in those red letters, He tells us that we must minister to sick people and to those in prison, feed the hungry and give water to the thirsty. Jesus also warned his listeners:

"Not everyone who says to me, `Lord, Lord,' will enter the kingdom of heaven, but only he who does the will of my Father who is in heaven. Many will say to me on that day, `Lord, Lord, did we not prophesy in your name, and in your name drive out demons and perform many miracles?' Then I will tell them plainly, `I never knew you. Away from me, you evildoers!' Matthew 7:21-23

What are you doing today?

Power Principle #28
The fear of the LORD motivates us to hate evil.

To fear the LORD is to hate evil; I hate pride and arrogance, evil behavior and perverse speech. Proverbs 8:13

If you want to know how much you love God, think about how you feel about the things that God hates, like: divorce, pornography, child abuse, homosexuality, sex outside of the marriage covenant, injustice in the courtroom, and abortion, to name just a few.

How do you feel about dishonest politicians and greedy lawyers who will sue anyone for anything in order to hit the jackpot? How do you feel about stem-cell research on aborted babies, or the fact that women are paid to have late term abortions so that the baby parts can be sold for big bucks? Does it bother you that Christians in Muslim and communist countries are rounded up like cattle, tortured and murdered? Does it bother you that juries are selected to ensure that the guilty go unpunished?

Would you vote for a presidential candidate who would appoint Supreme Court justices who support abortion, same sex marriage, and child pornography? Did you vote for President Clinton, who actually vetoed a law that would have outlawed partial birth abortions? If you did, then the blood of every innocent baby who has been slaughtered at the hands of an abortionist is on your head; and you need to fall on your face before God and beg for His mercy. James warns lukewarm Christians:

You adulterous people, don't you know that friendship with the world is hatred toward God? Anyone who chooses to be a friend of the world becomes an enemy of God. James 4:4

The bottom line is this. God hates evil. Do you?

Power Principle #29
The fear of the LORD replaces the fear of man.

Fear of man will prove to be a snare, but whoever trusts in the LORD is kept safe. Proverbs 29:25

If we are afraid of what man can do to us, then we will do the absolute opposite of what God wants us to do. For instance, I know a young Christian teacher who told me that she was going to join the anti-God teachers' union, because she was afraid that she might be blackballed if she didn't. Unbelievable! What would Christians in the old Soviet Union think? They risked their lives daily, when they chose not to join the atheistic communist party. Unfortunately, she is not the only one in the church who walks in the fear of man. When we fear what men think about us, we are paralyzed and polarized—basically, good for nothing in God's kingdom. The prophet Isaiah said:

The LORD spoke to me with his strong hand upon me, warning me not to follow the way of this people. He said: "Do not call conspiracy everything that these people call conspiracy; do not fear what they fear, and do not dread it. The LORD Almighty is the one you are to regard as holy, He is the One you are to fear, He is the One you are to dread, and he will be a sanctuary." Isaiah 8:11-14

Jesus is a sanctuary, a place of refuge, for those who fear the LORD and are living every day for the purposes of God. Are you living a God-centered purpose-driven life?

Power Principle #30
The fear of the LORD sets us apart to obey and serve God.

Then those who feared the LORD talked with each other, and the LORD listened and heard. A scroll of remembrance was written in his presence concerning those who feared the LORD and honored his name. "They will be mine," says the LORD Almighty, "in the day when I make up my treasured possession. I will spare them, just as in compassion a man spares his son who serves him. And you will again see the distinction between the righteous and the wicked, between those who serve God and those who do not. Malachi 3:16-18

The truth is, the fear of the LORD leads to obedience and righteous living. When we live to serve God and make decisions that are based upon pleasing Him rather than ourselves, we are different from the wicked who do not serve God. This is the simple dividing line between those who are saved and those who are lost.

Jesus is a perfect example of a life lived in the awesome reverence of a holy God. Because of His love for the Father, He was willing to leave His glorious home in heaven, experience every pain, grief, rejection, abandonment, and sorrow known to mankind, and suffer a tortuous death on a criminal's cross in order to fulfill God's purpose in the earth. His obedience brought glory to His heavenly Father.

The great news is that we, too, can bring glory to God by how we live. As we grow in our intimate knowledge of Him, our passion for Him will motivate us to do good, shun evil, and serve the One we love.

Power Principle #31
If you trust God, you will obey Him.

Many Christians are just plain scared to death to do anything that is outside of their comfort zone. Well, I've got news for you! Jesus is calling you out of your comfort zone—to a place where you must trust Him in order to be successful.

My son, if you accept my words and store up my commands within you, turning your ear to wisdom and applying your heart to understanding, and if you call out for insight and cry aloud for understanding, and if you look for it as for silver and search for it as for hidden treasure, the you will understand the fear of the LORD and find the knowledge of God. Proverbs 2:1-5

There is only one way to live a faith-filled victorious life: you must know God intimately. You must be able to trust God in order to live a life of obedience to His word, because His ways are not our ways. When He tells you to do something, it will not be what makes sense to most people.

For instance, it does not make sense to tithe. How can I give away a tenth of my income, if I do not believe that God will take care of my financial needs? I will not be obedient to God's requirement to tithe if I do not trust Him. The great news is that God has proven to me over and over again that His word is true: He is my provider, and He will never leave me nor forsake me.

By the way, if you want to know what God is like, just get to know Jesus. He and the Father are one.

Power Principle #32
The fear of the LORD leads to righteous living.

The LORD commanded us to obey all these decrees and to fear the LORD our God, so that we might always prosper and be kept alive, as is the case today. And if we are careful to obey all this law before the LORD our God, as he has commanded us, that will be our righteousness." Deuteronomy 6:24,25

God is love, and His kingdom is ruled by love; therefore, every commandment of God is rooted in love. For example, if you love God with all your heart, soul, mind and strength, you will automatically obey the first four commandments, which deal with our relationship with God:

- You will have no other gods in your life;
- You will not worship graven images;
- You will not take His name in vain;
- You will want to honor the Lord's day His way.

If you love others as yourself, then:
- You will honor your parents, regardless of how they treated you;
- You will not hate others, or abort your unborn child;
- You will not lie or gossip about others;
- You will not steal from anyone or envy what they have.

You will care about those who are suffering, and love will motivate you to reach out and minister to their needs. You will want to do good to others, rather than try to hurt them in any way.

Love is the litmus test of genuine Christianity. You cannot conjure it up or fake it. Unconditional love flows from God to His obedient children, those who have discovered the fear of the LORD. Like syrup on pancakes, love soaks the faithful servant of the Lord and then overflows to others. It is sweet to the taste and brings delight to all who eat of it.

> **Power Principle #33**
> *The fear of the LORD leads to true worship.*

Unfortunately, many Christians really believe that they have done their duty to God because they go to church on Sundays and sing in the choir. Well, that is not exactly true. True worship happens when we walk out the church door and go into our homes and the workplace. Genuine worship is when we lay down our lives, our time, our money, our plans and our agendas in order to please God. Sincere worship is obedience, and obedience requires sacrifice. A true worshipper is willing to give up something she treasures if God requires it.

Abraham was a sincere worshipper of God. We know that when God told him to sacrifice his son Isaac, he left his place of safety, took a three-day journey, built an altar, and bound his son. The Bible says that when he lifted his knife to slay him, the angel of the LORD called to him from heaven and told him:

"Do not lay a hand on the boy," he said. "Do not do anything to him. Now I know that you fear God, because you have not withheld from me your son, your only son." Genesis 22:12

The evidence that Abraham feared God was his willingness to obey God and sacrifice the greatest treasure of his heart, Isaac. God will always require us to lay down our Isaacs in order to please Him. It is part of *Worship 101*. The great news is that you cannot outgive God.

Power Principle #34
The seeds of sacrifice always bring forth a harvest of blessing
too numerous to count.

Isn't that what happened with Abraham? Truly, his descendants became as numerous as the stars in the sky and as the sand on the seashore because he obeyed God.

The fear of the LORD is pure, enduring forever. Psalms 19:9

That's right pure and enduring. It will be here when hell freezes over. So, don't you think this is a pretty important thing to be teaching in the church? Moses thought so. That is why he commanded the children of Israel:

Assemble the people--men, women and children, and the aliens living in your towns—so they can listen and learn to fear the LORD your God and follow carefully all the words of this law. Their children, who do not know this law, must hear it and learn to fear the LORD your God as long as you live in the land you are crossing the Jordan to possess." Deuteronomy 31:12,13

Moses was serious—in fact, he was passionate about the fear of the LORD. He understood that God requires obedience, because obedience brings forth a harvest of holiness. God is calling His children to understand the fear of the LORD, so that we obey Him and live a victorious life in Christ as royal servants in the King's court.

Points to Ponder...

- Are you in the habit of making serious decisions without counsel?
- Do you make excuses for not obeying the word of God?
- What is your concept of evil? Does it match up with God's?
- What does your schedule look like?
- Does your schedule leave time for serving others?
- Where do you spend most of your spare time?
- Are you willing to obey God even when you don't understand?

Quiet Time...

Dearest Heavenly Father,

Forgive me, Lord, for I have sinned against You, not only by the things I have done, but by the things that I have left undone. Lord, I am not content to live my life foolishly. I want to know Your ways and fulfill Your divine purpose for my life. Reveal to me the things that You love, and give me a pure hatred for the things You hate. Show me the truth about myself, so that I may repent and find forgiveness in Your sight. I just simply want to please You. I love You, Lord. I am Yours, and You are forever mine. *Amen.*

Does the LORD delight in burnt offerings and sacrifices as much as in obeying the voice of the LORD?
To obey is better than sacrifice, and to heed is better than the fat of rams.
1 Samuel 15:22

CHAPTER 10

The *Obstacle of Fear*

Even though I walk through the valley of the shadow of death, I will fear no evil, for you are with me; your rod and your staff, they comfort me. Psalms 23:4

D o you want to live a supernatural life—one that fulfills God's plans and purposes in the earth? Well, as in any worthwhile endeavor, there are obstacles to overcome—rivers to cross, giants to kill, enemies to conquer. Thank God that, for every obstacle and enemy, we have tools and weapons of warfare to guarantee victory.

> *One of the greatest obstacles to victory is **fear**— and I mean, the wrong kind of fear!*

As we discovered before, there is a Godly fear—fear that comes from wisdom— the kind of fear that led Noah to obey God and build the ark to save his family from the coming judgment of God upon the wickedness of man:

*By faith Noah, when warned about things not yet seen, **in holy fear** built an ark to save his family. Hebrews 11:7*

The fear of the Lord is holy, and it motivates us to obey God, especially when God doesn't make sense. The Lord told Noah to get ready for the coming judgment. He gave him instructions and architectural drawings to build a ship that could hold a zoo. Noah believed God, so he started to work right away. For a hundred years, he tried to convince everyone else to forsake their sins and live, but they would not listen to him.

Can you imagine what everyone thought about this crazy man who was building a huge vessel in a place where there was no body of water big enough for it to float on? I am sure they thought he was a fool. After all, Noah and his sons could have been busy building their businesses instead of that boat. Thank God for all of us that Noah wasn't too concerned about what others thought of him—he might have decided that God wasn't all that serious about a flood. He might have decided to drag his feet. He might have missed the boat!

There is, however, a fear that causes men to stumble, to fall into disobedience against God's divine law of love, and to miss the mark where the treasures of His kingdom are hidden. Our fears come in many packages: fear of failure, fear of poverty, fear of sickness, fear of rejection, fear of the dark—fear of the truth! These fears and others are stumbling blocks on the path to a victorious and successful life in Christ—one that fulfills God's plans and purposes for our lives. Just take a look at the Israelites in the desert.

Moses told the Joshua generation what had happened when their parents, the Israelites, faced the decision of a lifetime! God had promised these former slaves from Egypt a land flowing with milk and honey, with fields and vineyards ready to harvest, with houses and cities ready to occupy—all they had to do was obey God: go in and take the land from its idol-worshipping inhabitants! Listen to Moses as he recounts the events surrounding their rebellion:

But you were unwilling to go up; you rebelled against the command of the LORD your God. You grumbled in your tents and said, "The LORD hates us; so, he brought us out of Egypt to deliver us into the hands of the Amorites to destroy us. Where can we go? Our brothers have made us lose heart. They say, `The people are stronger and taller than we are; the cities are large, with walls up to the sky. We even saw the Amorites there.' "
Deuteronomy 1:26-28

Then I said to you, **"Do not be terrified; do not be afraid of them.** *The LORD your God,*
who is going before you, will fight for you, as he did for you in Egypt, before your very eyes,
and in the desert. There you saw how the LORD your God carried you, as a father carries
his son, all the way you went until you reached this place." In spite of this, you did not trust in
the LORD your God, who went ahead of you on your journey, in fire by night and in a cloud
by day, to search out places for you to camp and to show you the way you should go.
Deuteronomy 1:29-33

When the LORD heard what you said, he was angry and solemnly swore: "Not a man of
this evil generation shall see the good land I swore to give your forefathers, except Caleb son
of Jephunneh. He will see it, and I will give him and his descendants the land he set his feet
on, because he followed the LORD wholeheartedly."
Deuteronomy 1:34-36

What was wrong with these people? God had miraculously delivered them from the
mightiest army in the civilized world and had left Egypt in shambles. The Israelites did
not lift a finger on their own behalf. God did it all—with various kinds of judgments and
plagues—and even caused them to walk through a river on dry land. He fed them with
"angel food" and quenched their thirst with water from a rock. What was their problem?

Through close examination, I have determined that these people had severe health
problems. Yes, my friends—serious problems with their eyes, ears, mind, and heart. First,
let's discuss the *vision* problem: it is obvious that they had a problem with their *focus*. You
see, rather than focusing on the awesome power of God, which they had seen in His
dealings with Egypt, they saw the inhabitants of the land as bigger than God. In
addition, the Israelites focused inwardly—they were depending upon their own strength
to defeat the enemy, rather than looking toward their Commander-in-Chief, the
Almighty God.

The Israelites also had a *hearing* problem. Rather than listening to the good report of
Joshua and Caleb, or even to Moses' words of encouragement, they only *heard the*
negative report of the other ten spies. They had a serious problem with selective hearing.

The Israelites also had a *hearing* problem. Rather than listening to the good report of Joshua and Caleb, or even to Moses' words of encouragement, they only *heard the* negative report of the other ten spies. They had a serious problem with selective hearing.

Now, let's talk about the problem with their *minds*. The Israelites' mindset was that of a slave. The whole nation had been captive to the Egyptians for over 400 years. Before their deliverance from Egypt, they had no rights to life, liberty, or the pursuit of happiness—and they had fallen into idol worship. There was no Bible or Torah, because Moses had not written it yet. They had no law of God, because God had not given it yet. Other than bedtime stories about their ancestors, they had no *knowledge of God*—and they had no tabernacle,
priesthood, or sacrificial system. However, they did *know* the wicked ways of the Egyptians and their idol-worshipping practices. Their minds had not been renewed: although God had revealed His awesome power to them, they chose to *think* like a slave rather than a child of God.

The Israelites also had a *heart* problem. They were very ungrateful and full of anger towards God. They made serious charges against God and Moses as they grumbled in their tents. Rather than thanking God for bringing them to the promised land and providing their every need along the way, they called their travel agency to make plans to return home to slavery.

The end result was their stubborn refusal to go with God—they said no to God and never entered into the promise. Instead, they were consigned to wander in the desert for forty years.

> *We have a tendency to be a lot like these stubborn Israelites until we learn to trust in the Lord.*

In the New Testament, it appears that the apostle Peter continued to have a problem with *fear*. We know what he did on the night Jesus was betrayed; because of *the fear of man,* Peter denied that he was Jesus' disciple. However, on the Day of Pentecost, he became a *fearless* preacher of the Gospel, which put him in physical danger. Yet even great men of God like Peter battle with the flesh. Sometime later, the apostle Paul reprimanded Peter for his sin of hypocrisy that came as a result of fear:

When Peter came to Antioch, I opposed him to his face, because he was clearly in the wrong. Before certain men came from James, he used to eat with the Gentiles. But when they arrived, he began to draw back and separate himself from the Gentiles because he was afraid of those who belonged to the circumcision group. The other Jews joined him in his hypocrisy, so that by their hypocrisy even Barnabas was led astray. Galatians 2:11-13

Power Principle #35
The fear of man will always cause you to sin against God.

Fear of man will prove to be a snare, but whoever trusts in the LORD is kept safe. Proverbs 29:25

The Bible is full of stories of courageous men and women who *feared God* more than man, including these two ancient nurses:

The king of Egypt said to the Hebrew midwives, whose names were Shiphrah and Puah, "When you help the Hebrew women in childbirth and observe them on the delivery stool, if it is a boy, kill him; but if it is a girl, let her live." The midwives, however, feared God and did not do what the king of Egypt had told them to do; they let the boys live. Then the king of Egypt summoned the midwives and asked them, "Why have you done this? Why have you let the boys live?" Exodus 1:15-18

The midwives answered Pharaoh, "Hebrew women are not like Egyptian women; they are vigorous and give birth before the midwives arrive." So, God was kind to the midwives and the people increased and became even more numerous. And because the midwives feared God, He gave them families of their own. Exodus 1:19-21

Today, *fear* leads women to abort and kill their own unborn babies. *Afraid* of the future, *afraid* to lose a boyfriend or husband, *afraid* of her parents' response to an unwed pregnancy—a woman is deceived. She believes and acts upon the lie that an abortion will solve her problems, only to find out that her sorrows are magnified.

What a difference between those who *fear man* vs. those who *fear God*. In spite of Pharaoh's decree that all male infants be killed, Moses' mother and father courageously protected their beautiful baby boy, which put them in great danger.

By faith, Moses' parents hid him for three months after he was born, because they saw he was no ordinary child, and they were not afraid of the King's edict. Hebrews 11:23

Moses persevered and fulfilled God's purpose for his life because he had perfect *vision*. He *saw* the invisible God and His awesome power as greater than the hand of Pharaoh, and the treasures of His Kingdom as more valuable than the possessions, power, popularity, and pleasure found in Pharaoh's palace.

By faith Moses, when he had grown up, refused to be known as the son of Pharaoh's daughter. He chose to be mistreated along with the people of God rather than to enjoy the pleasures of sin for a short time. He regarded disgrace for the sake of Christ as of greater value than the treasures of Egypt, because he was looking ahead to his reward. By faith he left Egypt, not fearing the king's anger; he persevered because he saw him who is invisible. Hebrews 11:24-27 How can we avoid the obstacle of fear and stay on the straight and narrow path that leads to life, victory, and blessing—a life that fulfills God's purposes on Earth? We must have corrected *vision*! We must *see* God to *know* Him—who He really is—so that we can learn to *trust* Him.

> *Webster says...*
>
> *Trust:*
> - *Assured reliance on the character, ability, strength or truth of someone or something;*
> - *To place confidence in;*
> - *To rely upon;*
> - *To believe;*
> - *To hope;*
> - *To commit or place in one's care or keeping.*

The New Testament calls us to place our **trust** or **faith** in the person of Jesus Christ, the truth of His teaching, and the redemptive work He accomplished at Calvary. The result of faith in Jesus is a radical, total commitment to Him as the Lord of one's life.

Like the Israelites, we too must have **heart** surgery. The apostle Peter says:

*Who is going to harm you if you are eager to do good? But even if you should suffer for what is right, you are blessed. "Do not fear what they fear; do not be frightened." But in your **hearts** set apart Christ as Lord. 1 PE 3:13-15*

We do not have to fear what everyone else fears. When Jesus is Lord of your life, you can rest assured that:

- No weapon formed against you by man will prosper.
- All things work together for good for you, because you are living to fulfill God's purpose for your life.
- God will supply all of your needs according to His great riches.
- He is the Great Physician who heals you.
- His mercies are new every morning.
- You are accepted among the brethren.
- You are His precious possession.

As a child of God, you can pray as the psalmist did:

*Teach me your way, O LORD, and I will walk in your truth; give me an undivided heart, that I may **fear** Your name. Psalm 86:11*

---

*Rather than making choices and decisions based upon **fear**, we have the power to make the right decisions*
—God's will, not our own—
based upon our confidence in Him to lead and direct our steps.

Trust in the Lord with all your heart and lean not on your own understanding; in all your ways acknowledge him, and he will make your paths straight. Proverbs 3:5-6

We live every day, placing our faith in lots of people and things, people we do not even know. We trust airline pilots and mechanics, air traffic controllers and equipment, every time we board a plane. We trust other drivers every time we get into the family car to go somewhere. We entrust our bodies to food manufacturers, physicians, hospitals, pharmaceutical companies, and the FDA *(Food and Drug Administration)*. We entrust our children to schools, teachers, youth pastors, moviemakers, the television studios, and friends—all very unreliable, to say the least.

Are you willing to entrust your life to the Maker of the Universe? It becomes a lot easier to do so when you personally know His love, His character, and Who He really is. God's desire is for each of His children to come close—not like the Israelites, who were afraid of the presence of God and sent Moses to be the messenger go-between. He wants you to draw near to Him, cuddle up, smell His fragrance, and hear His heartbeat. He wants you to dwell in the shelter of the Most High God and rest in the shadow of the Almighty. He wants to be your refuge and fortress, the One you trust. He wants to save you from the *fowler's snare* and from the deadly pestilence.

During biblical times, a *fowler* was bird-catcher who caught his prey by trickery. God wants to save you from your enemy, the devil who tries to ensnare you through deception and trickery to bring you to ruin. Like a mother eagle protects her young by covering them under the comfort of her huge wings, so God desires to be your safe harbor. Can you say with confidence that:

God is our refuge and strength, an ever-present help in trouble. Therefore, we will not ***fear****, though the earth give way and the mountains fall into the heart of the sea, though its waters roar and foam and the mountains quake with their surging. Psalm 46:1-3*

As hurricanes, tornadoes, and floods overtake cities, forest fires devour homes, earthquakes shake the foundations of buildings and roads, and terrorists spread fear throughout the earth, can you say with confidence that:

The LORD is a refuge for the oppressed, a stronghold in times of trouble. Those who know Your name will trust in You, for you, LORD, have never forsaken those who seek you. Psalm 9:9-10

Jesus tells us that we can know this God and trust Him.

"Do not let your hearts be troubled. Trust in God; trust also in me. In my Father's house are many rooms; if it were not so, I would have told you. I am going there to prepare a place for you. And if I go and prepare a place for you, I will come back and take you to be with me that you also may be where I am. You know the way to the place where I am going." John 14:1-4

Thomas said to him, "Lord, we don't know where you are going, so how can we know the way?" Jesus answered, "I am the way and the truth and the life. No one comes to the Father except through me. If you really knew me, you would know my Father as well. From now on, you do know Him and have seen Him. Philip said, "Lord, show us the Father and that will be enough for us." John 14:5-8

Jesus answered: "Don't you know me, Philip, even after I have been among you such a long time? Anyone who has seen me has seen the Father. How can you say, `Show us the Father? Don't you believe that I am in the Father, and that the Father is in me? The words I say to you are not just my own. Rather, it is the Father, living in me, who is doing his work. Believe me when I say that I am in the Father and the Father is in me; or at least believe on the evidence of the miracles themselves. John 14:9-11

God's Word is true and faithful. He promises that:

*Good will come to him who is generous and lends freely, who conducts his affairs with justice. Surely, he will never be shaken; a righteous man will be remembered forever. He will have no fear of bad news; his heart is steadfast, trusting in the LORD. His heart is secure, he will have **no fear**; in the end he will look in triumph on his foes. Psalm 112:5-8*

You know, the media is full of bad news—news that brings terror and fear to the hearts of millions of viewers. Every day, millions of men and women get drunk, take drugs or tranquilizers in an attempt to bring peace of mind and heart. God's word gives us the only prescription for true and lasting peace.

You will keep in perfect peace him whose mind is steadfast, because he trusts in You. Trust in the Lord forever, for the Lord, the Lord, is the Rock Eternal. Isaiah 26:3,4

How was Esther, a young Jewish woman, able to walk into the lion's den when she went to see the King? Esther had put her trust in the only One who could save her life and her nation.

"But blessed is the man who trust in the Lord, whose confidence is in Him. He will be like a tree planted by the water that sends out its roots by the stream. It does not fear when heat comes; its leaves are always green. It has no worries in a year of drought and never fails to bear fruit." Jeremiah 17:7,8

Points to Ponder…

- What are you afraid of?
- When confronted with difficult circumstances, what do you focus on?
- When confronted with difficult circumstances, whom do you depend upon for the answers?
- In the midst of a trial, do you listen to the "experts" or God's word?
- Do your thoughts line up with God's word?
- Are you grateful for all of God's blessings in your life? Are you in the habit of giving Him thanks, even when times are difficult?
- Have you made a conscious decision to surrender your life into the hands of God?

Quiet Time…

Dearest Heavenly Father,

Forgive me for being anxious and fearful over so many issues—too many to mention, but I'm sure You know about them all. I desire the peace that passes all understanding, the peace that washes over me regardless of my circumstances. I want to know what it is like to live under the shadow of Your wing, to live under the shelter of the Almighty. Lord, help me to let go of all that I treasure and hold dear to my heart so that I might take Your hand and go where You lead. Deliver me from all of my fears. I love You, Lord. I am Yours, and You are forever mine. *Amen.*

May the God of hope fill you with all joy and peace as you trust in Him, so that you may overflow with hope by the power of the Holy Spirit.
Romans 15:13

Webster says...

Follow:
- *To go, proceed, or come after;*
- *To pursue in an effort to overtake;*
- *To accept as authority;*
- *To obey;*
- *To copy or imitate;*
- *To engage in as a calling or way of life;*

CHAPTER 11

The *Cross*

Blessed are they whose ways are blameless, who walk according to the law of the Lord. Blessed are they who keep his statutes and seek him with all their heart. They do nothing wrong; they walk in His ways. PS 119:1-3

As we seek to fulfill our divine destiny—royal service in the King's court—we learn to trust in His wisdom and His love for us. We make mistakes along the way, fall down get scraped up a bit, and wander off the beaten path. All the while, Jesus is the Good Shepherd who chases after us, binds up our wounds, comforts us, and gets us back on track. Gradually, we learn some lessons—like the one about doing it His way.

Before embarking upon a journey, the wise traveler will generally have a map and will plot the path to be taken. The experienced traveler will go to someone who has already made the journey to discover any hidden dangers or trouble spots along the way. Like the early pioneers of the great west, our journey through life is so treacherous that we must be guided through the danger zones—to attempt the journey alone would guarantee disaster, and we would perish along the way. Thank God, we have Jesus, who has already walked the "way of the Lord". The great news is that He now calls us to *follow* Him.

*As Jesus was walking beside the Sea of Galilee, he saw two brothers, Simon called Peter and his brother Andrew. They were casting a net into the lake, for they were fishermen. "Come, **follow Me**," Jesus said, "and I will make you fishers of men." At once they left their nets and **followed Him**. Matthew 4:18-20*

Jesus called His disciples to leave their way of life, their treasures, their business ventures to *follow Him*. Did they fully comprehend what Jesus was calling them to do?

Jesus is calling us to *come after* Him, to *pursue* and *overtake* Him. In other words, we are to *chase* after Him until we *capture* and *possess* Him as our very own. However, this creates a problem for most people, because most people are busy *chasing* other things—things like possessions, power, prestige, pleasure, popularity—the pride of life and the lusts of the eyes.

The fact of the matter is that we can only chase after one thing at a time. Can you imagine how confusing it would be for a hunting dog to chase after three deer at a time? He would be running around in circles for days. Isn't that a picture of life? We chase after the glitz and glitter of this world like a dog chasing his tail, and we end our days in sorrow. No. We have a better choice before us—we can choose to *chase* after Jesus, who gives us the desires of our hearts and fills our life with all that is good.

Jesus is also calling us to accept Him as the *absolute authority* in our lives. This poses another problem for most people in our society today. We are born to be rebellious. No one really wants to be told what to do—just look at two-year-olds and teenagers. But it doesn't end there—the prisons are full of those who refuse to obey those in authority.

In reality, we are all lawbreakers and criminals, because we have all broken God's royal law of love as outlined in the Ten Commandments. That is why we needed a Savior— one who was able to completely obey God's law of love and then take our punishment for sin. It is only when we receive Jesus Christ into our lives as *Lord and Savior* that we are able to *obey* Him, *imitate* Him, and *engage* in His way of life. He will lead us to the place of fulfillment of God's purpose for our lives in the same way that He did—the *way of the cross*.

*Then Jesus said to his disciples, "If anyone would come after me, he must **deny** himself and take up his **cross** and **follow me**." Matthew 16:24*

> *Webster's says:*
> *Deny: to restrain oneself from gratification of desires*

The *cross* is an instrument of execution. Jesus is calling us to *deny* and *put to death* the desires of the flesh *(our sinful nature)* in order that we might walk in full obedience to the will of God. There is no other way. The sinful nature is diabolically opposed to God. The person who lives according to the flesh is an *enemy of God* and a *friend of Satan.*

Jesus is very serious about this issue. He says:

"If your right eye causes you to sin, gouge it out and throw it away. It is better for you to lose one part of your body than for your whole body to be thrown into hell. And if your right hand causes you to sin, cut it off and throw it away. It is better for you to lose one part of your body than for your whole body to go into hell." Matthew 5:29,30

Amputation is a serious issue—and yet, that is exactly how Jesus says we must treat sin. Is it possible that our sweet Savior could really mean what He says? Call it shock treatment, but I believe He is telling us to get serious about sin in our lives. Like the surgical removal of skin during circumcision, we are to cut off and remove from our lives anything that would cause us to sin.

For example, if you have a problem with Internet pornography, get rid of your computer! How hard is that? Okay, maybe sexual perversion isn't your thing. Maybe you have a problem with gluttony—yes, excessive eating of all the wrong foods seems to be the prevalent sin among American Christians—and it is sin. If so, don't visit buffet restaurants, don't purchase junk foods, stay away from fast food restaurants, buy plenty of fresh veggies and fruits, no cookies, candy or ice cream—and fast once or twice a week until you get rid of that demon.

Maybe you do not have time to clean your house, prepare healthy meals, help others, read your Bible or spend time with God in prayer because you are addicted to soap operas or romance novels. This one is pretty simple—get rid of the television and don't buy any more romance novels.

Maybe you have a problem with handling money. You like to play the lottery, you are hooked on Internet shopping, and you cannot pay all of the credit card bills that are piling up, because you can't seem to live within your means. My, my—greed is an ugly sin. Get rid of the credit cards and debit cards, get on a budget, start tithing, and make Jesus Lord of your finances. If your spouse can't handle money either, give your checkbook and bills to an honest friend who can give you an allowance and pay your bills for you. How hard is that? Well, the truth is, unless you want to please God more than yourself, it won't happen. Jesus tells us that:

*"Anyone who loves his father or mother more than me is not worthy of me; anyone who loves his son or daughter more than me is not worthy of me; and anyone who does not take his **cross** and **follow me** is not worthy of me. Whoever finds his life will lose it, and whoever loses his life for my sake will find it. Matthew 10:37-39*

Jesus hits us right where it hurts, because for most people on planet Earth, family is our most treasured possession. Jesus is saying that He will have no idols before Him —not our parents, our children, nor ourselves! He requires absolute loyalty. In fact, there is no room for #2 in the disciple's life. This is the meaning of true commitment. Luke tells us that:

*Large crowds were traveling with Jesus and turning to them he said: "If anyone comes to me and does not hate his father and mother, his wife and children, his brothers and sisters —yes, even his own life—he cannot be my disciple. And anyone who does not carry his **cross** and **follow Me** cannot be my disciple." Luke 14:25-27*

Can you imagine anyone but Jesus saying something like that? Think about it. By this time in His ministry, He has a large crowd that follows Him as He travels from town to town. People leave their jobs to hike down the highway with this itinerant preacher, hoping to see another miracle or get a free lunch. Jesus is not impressed with His massive following—He knows the condition of their hearts and warns the people about the seriousness of commitment.

Does Jesus really mean that we are to hate our family members as well as ourselves? No—because we are required to love everyone, including our parents and children and other family members. However, we must be willing to give up everything, including our own families and our lives, if necessary, for the purposes of God. That is reality for Christians in Muslim and Hindu cultures. When Muslims and Hindus are converted to Christ, their families usually disown them. Many are put to death by their own parents and relatives. Consider Chinese Christians, who risk their lives daily for the sake of the Gospel; and Christians in North Korea, where owning a Bible is a capital offense worthy of the death penalty. Truly, for these saints, to embrace Christ is to embrace the *cross*.

Modern day martyrs abound throughout the world today:

- Li Ying, a young Chinese woman, is serving a 15-year prison sentence for the "crime" of printing a Christian magazine.

- Two young men, Tapan Roy, 27, and Liplal Marandi, 21, were attacked and killed by radical Muslims for sharing the gospel in a small village south of Dhaka, Bangladesh. They had been showing the *JESUS* film; and when they refused to stop, the Islamic religious leader sent a mob to kill them while they slept.

- Pastor Y, who lives on the island of Java in Indonesia, was disowned by his parents and expelled from his home at the age of 22, when he became a Christian. When he and his wife brought a 16-year-old Muslim girl to Christ, they were arrested, accused of kidnapping, and spent four years in prison.

- Gulnaz Bibi, a 17-year-old Pakistani girl angered a Muslim man when she rejected his advances. Her body and face were completely disfigured by the acid that he threw at her as an act of revenge.

- Javed Anjum, a 20-year-old Pakistani was tortured for five days in 2004. His fingers were broken, and his fingernails were ripped out.

- In Bangladesh, Christian converts' homes are burned and their families attacked.

- Pastor Stephen, the pastor of a pioneering church in the northern part of Bangladesh, has a school for over 120 Muslim and Hindu children, where they receive a free education and a meal for the day. On December 31, 2004, he was returning home in the evening, when three unidentified men attacked him. They stabbed him indiscriminately in his abdomen and all over his body. They shot him eight times in the face with a shotgun. Miraculously, he survived the attack because villagers rushed him to the hospital for surgery, where they removed 100 of the 240 pellets in his face.

- Santosa, a farmer and pastor of a small village church in the small town of Poso of Indonesia, was attacked by machete wielding Muslims. The attacker missed his throat but cut him across his face. His tongue was slashed, and he lost ten teeth in the process. He says, "God sends me power so I can bear the suffering. We rejoice that one Muslim has come to Christ." *(The Voice of the Martyrs, October 2005)*

Even now, three beautiful Christian women in Indonesia, Eti Pangesti, Dr. Rebekka Loanita and Ratna Malabangun, have been sentenced to three years in prison for the "crime" of teaching Sunday school. Would you teach Sunday school if it held the risk of sending you to prison? One of these women, Dr. Rebekka, is a physician. Would you risk losing your career—one that costs you eight years of college, internship and residency—in order to teach Sunday school to little children?

How many churches in America are filled with people who really believe they have a ticket to heaven—people who are unwilling to deny self, much less give up family or their own lives. Jesus says these people do not qualify to be called His disciples—they cannot fulfill God's purpose for their lives on Earth. What about you? Do you qualify? What would you be *unwilling* to sacrifice in order to be called a disciple of Jesus Christ?

Power Principle #36
*True worship requires personal **sacrifice**.*

We must be willing to *sacrifice (give up, deny self)* anything that God requires of us, especially the acts of our sinful nature. The apostle Paul gives us a list of nasty, ugly sinful attitudes and actions that no serious Christian would want in their lives:

The acts of the sinful nature are obvious: sexual immorality, impurity and debauchery; idolatry and witchcraft; hatred, discord, jealousy, fits of rage, selfish ambition, dissensions, factions and envy; drunkenness, orgies, and the like. I warn you, as I did before, that those who live like this will not inherit the Kingdom of God. Galatians 5:19-21

Paul warns us that those who live according to the sinful nature will not inherit the Kingdom of God. This is a serious business. Sin is serious business, because God is serious about sin. Get the picture? So, if God is so serious about sin, why do we have sexual immorality in the church? Why are so many Christians filled with greed, which is the sin of idolatry? Why is there hatred and discord in Christian marriages? Why are the sins of bitterness and unforgiveness rampant in the church? Why do Christians envy those in the workplace who get promoted instead of them? Why do so many Christians seek after position, prestige, power and popularity—all the result of selfish ambition? Is it because we do not see these things as sin? Do we believe we can live according to the sinful desires of the flesh and ever please God? Are we relying on "once saved, always saved" as our ticket out of hell?

> *Paul warns us that those who live according to the sinful nature will **not** inherit the Kingdom of God!*

Listen to Paul's warning, and if necessary, repent—turn away from these acts of the sinful nature and live according to the Spirit of God, which is love. Paul gives us a description of love—what love looks like in the life of a believer:

But the fruit of the Spirit is love, joy, peace, patience, kindness, goodness, faithfulness, gentleness and self-control. Against such things there is no law. Those who belong to Christ Jesus have crucified the sinful nature with its passions and desires. Galatians 5:22-25

In other words, if you love God with your whole heart, soul, mind and strength, and love your neighbor in the same way that God loves you, then your life will be characterized by:

- Joy, regardless of your circumstances.
- Peace of mind and heart, even if the world is falling apart.
- Patience, in your own life and with others.
- Kindness towards those whom you love and those who hate you.
- Goodness lived out in acts of mercy.
- Faithfulness, honoring your word even when it hurts.
- Gentleness in word and deed; and,
- Self-control, able to live a disciplined lifestyle according to the Word of God.

Does this describe you? I know that we are not perfect, we are all a work in progress; but are you growing in the fruit of the Spirit? If not, then there several things that you must do to promote growth:

- First, you must fertilize your spiritual life by putting to death the acts of the sinful nature. As you crucify the sinful nature, it can be used as spiritual compost to bring forth the nature of Christ, the fruit of the Spirit of God.

- Next, you must do some weeding in the garden of your heart—pull up the weeds of unforgiveness and the roots of bitterness that are choking the love of God. Oh, and don't forget to pull up the deceit of riches and the cares of this world that choke the Word of God.

- Next, you must water the garden of your heart with time spent in God's word and in praise and prayer. It is in His presence that we are changed from glory to glory.

- And finally, you must shine the light of good works as you give of your time, attention, and resources to help others in need.

The unconditional love of God, flowing to and through a believer, creates a new and beautiful example of the grace of God. Because God is love, we are able to love others in the same way that He loves us.

The apostle John was a man who knew the love of Jesus in a most intimate way. Like a child, he was willing and able to cuddle up to Jesus, and he was called "the disciple whom Jesus loved". He wrote about this great love of God when he said:

Dear friends, let us love one another, for love comes from God. Everyone who loves has been born of God and knows God. Whoever does not love does not know God, because God is love. This is how God showed his love among us: He sent his one and only Son into the world that we might live through him. This is love: not that we loved God,

---

but that he loved us and sent his Son as an atoning sacrifice for our sins. Dear friends, since God so loved us, we also ought to love one another. No one has ever seen God; but if we love one another, God lives in us and his love is made complete in us. 1 John 4:7-12

For the serious believer, the one who aspires to royal service in the King's court, Jesus says:

*The man who loves his life will lose it, while the man who hates his life in this world will keep it for eternal life. Whoever serves me must follow me; and where I am, my servant also will be. **My Father will honor the one who serves me.** John 12:25,26*

Points to Ponder…

- Have you made the decision to chase after Jesus and His kingdom? Why or why not?
- Have you made Jesus and His word the ultimate authority in your life? Why or why not?
- Is there any area of sin in your life that you are struggling with?
- Are you willing to surrender this area of your life to the lordship of Jesus Christ?
- Are you really serious about crucifying sinful attitudes in your life, such as an ungrateful spirit, jealousy, envy, bitterness, and unforgiveness?
- Are you growing in the fruit of the Holy Spirit?
- Do you love others in the same way that God loves you?
- How much of Jesus do you really want?

Quiet Time...

Dearest Heavenly Father,

I confess that, at times, I make excuses for my sinful attitudes and actions. I have failed to see my sin through Your holy eyes, and I have grieved the Holy Spirit. I have not taken captive my desires to pursue personal gain and pleasure, rather than pursuing You and Your love. In addition, I have failed to show forth Your love to those around me. Please forgive me and change my heart. Give me Your unconditional love for others, so that I may reach out in royal service to you. I love You, Lord. I am Yours, and You are forever mine. **Amen.**

You have laid down precepts that are to be fully obeyed.
Oh, that my ways were steadfast in obeying your decrees! Then I would not be put to
shame when I consider all your commands.
PS 119:4-6

CHAPTER 12

The *Royal Romance*

Take me away with you—let us hurry! Let the king bring me into his chambers. We rejoice and delight in you; we will praise your love more than wine. Song of Songs 1:4

Every little girl loves to listen to bedtime stories that tell about the handsome prince who rescues the fair maiden from evil and carries her off to his castle to live happily ever after. Dressed in a magnificent gown and crowned with jewels, the fair maiden is transformed into a beautiful princess. A gala ball is held to celebrate the royal marriage, and they live happily ever after in wedded bliss, free from the trials and tragedies of real life. For a moment in time, even the poorest or homeliest child imagines herself in the arms of her prince as they begin their waltz of life.

Well, I am here to tell you some great news. You are invited to a royal banquet and wedding feast to be held at the royal residence of the King of Kings—and you will be joined to the Prince of Peace in holy matrimony! On top of all of that, you will live together for eternity, free from all sickness, disease, tragedy, sorrow, and death. There will be no more war, no more grief, no more tears—forever and ever and ever, Amen. Incredible as it seems, that is God's plan for each of His royal children.

Now, it is customary for a couple that wants to get married to have one thing in common; they love each other. Certainly, our storybook characters are in love, and they want to be together, forsaking all others, in happily ever after land. The same is true with the wedding feast of the Lamb. *Love* is the ingredient necessary for admittance into this royal event.

Now, let's discuss this divine love—the kind of love that surpasses all others. Unlike divine love, human love does not endure that is why people fall in and out of love like the ocean's tide. A husband loves his wife as long as she performs according to his needs and wants. His love of golf or fishing may be greater than his love for his wife and children, which is why he will spend his spare time with his buddies on the golf course or on the river rather than spend time with his family. A wife may love her husband as long as he brings home the bacon and gives her the attention she needs—or she may love her children more than her husband and neglect him and his needs. Marriages fall apart because it is very difficult to love someone who is harsh, demanding, selfish, inconsiderate, argumentative, or shows very little love in return. Human love does not endure forever and ever. In Paul's second letter to Timothy, he describes the kind of love we see today:

*But mark this: There will be terrible times in **the last days**. People will be lovers of themselves, lovers of money, boastful, proud, abusive, disobedient to their parents, ungrateful, unholy, without love, unforgiving, slanderous, without self-control, brutal, not lovers of the good, treacherous, rash, conceited, lovers of pleasure rather than lovers of God—having a form of godliness but denying its power. Have nothing to do with them. 2 Timothy 3:1-5*

Most people, even Christian couples, get married for all of the wrong reasons. For instance, some get married for financial security, for companionship, for romance, for sex, for self-esteem, to name just a few. Basically, each person marries the other in the hope that his or her own needs will be met. The foundation of this marriage is cracked each time an expectation is unmet. For instance, if I *expect* my husband to meet my emotional need—which only God is capable of doing—then my love is strained and eventually will crack. If my husband *expects* me to have sex with him every single night, how is he going to feel if I'm just too tired or sick? What if I don't want to have sex with him because he was harsh with me earlier in the day? How is his "love" going to handle that?

Power Principle #37
Selfish human love cannot withstand the onslaught. of unmet expectations.

There is only one kind of love that can withstand the storms of life—a love that endures forever and ever and ever throughout eternity—God's *agape love*. This love flows forth—like a river from its source—from the very heart of God, because *He is agape love*. God's love for us is undeserved. In fact, we have done everything but slap Him in the face by our sinful attitudes and actions. We have done absolutely nothing to earn it, yet His love for us is deeper than the deepest ocean and reaches the highest heavens. The psalmist wrote of this great love when he said:

For as high as the heavens are above the earth, so great is his love for those who fear him; as far as the east is from the west, so far has he removed our transgressions from us. Psalm 103:11,12

What a wonderful promise for those who fear Him, who live to please Him through royal service in the King's court. In spite of our sins, he forgives us and removes our sins from us, so that we can enter into holy communion *(intimacy)* with Him. What kind of love is this that pays so dearly? In his letter to the Roman church, Paul tells us about this unselfish, life-giving, undeserved love:

You see, at just the right time, when we were still powerless, Christ died for the ungodly. Very rarely will anyone die for a righteous man, though for a good man someone might possibly dare to die. But God demonstrates his own love for us in this: While we were still sinners, Christ died for us. Romans 5:6-8

How true it is—very rarely will someone possibly die to save a good man. Yet, Jesus Christ died for us while we were still enemies of God—partakers of Satan's rebellion against God's royal kingdom.

What kind of love is this? What would compel God the Father, the Son and the Holy Spirit to agree to such a thing as this—that the Son of God would humble Himself, leave the glories of Heaven to become a part of His creation in the form of a helpless little child and die a torturous death on a Roman cross? Only His unfailing love and His desire to restore a fallen and sinful race back to Himself— that was the motivation for His great plan of salvation and redemption.

> *God wants to populate Heaven and Earth with His victorious children— those who have chosen to become servants in His royal kingdom of love.*

God's love will not fail—it will endure forever in the hearts of those who know, love and trust Him. This royal romance reveals His unfailing love that draws us to our eternal and divine destiny in Him.

"In your unfailing love you will lead the people you have redeemed. In your strength you will guide them to your holy dwelling. Exodus 15:13

Now, imagine that you are that fair maiden in our storybook romance. You have been redeemed from the magic curse of the evil sorcerer by the unconditional love of your prince charming. He fought the battle on your behalf and won the victory. You have been set free from the bondage and darkness of an endless night, and now you have a choice. Will you join your hero as he heads back to the castle, or will you remain in your world of mishap to face other dragons alone?

The fact is, this story is a picture of all that Jesus did for us. We were born into captivity, enslaved to sin and the prince of darkness. We were blind from birth, unaware of our own peril. Like the passengers on the Titanic, we had no idea as to the destruction that awaited us. Yet God, in His mercy, came to our defense, fought the battle that would set us free from captivity, and won the prize that was set before Him—a bride without spot or blemish. Are you willing to ride with Him to His holy dwelling? If so, then God has some promises for you. First of all, how would you like to be surrounded by God's unfailing love? The psalmist says:

Many are the woes of the wicked, but the LORD's unfailing love surrounds the man who trusts in him. Psalm 32:10

I don't know about you, but it gives me peace of mind to know that no weapon formed by man against me shall prosper, because God's unfailing love surrounds me like armor. My husband and I have experienced this love as we have faced trials in our home, our church and our business. It was God's unfailing love that restored our children, provided for us financially, and rescued us from false accusations and threats of imprisonment for something that we did not do *(Read "From Trials to Triumph")*. Our only hope was in His unfailing love and the knowledge that the eyes of the Lord were watching over us during our times of trial.

But the eyes of the LORD are on those who fear him, on those whose hope is in his unfailing love. Psalm 33:18

It doesn't matter who you are, what your education or background is, whether rich or poor, or where you are in your walk with God. Because of His unfailing love, you can find shelter and refuge under the shadow of His wings.

How priceless is your unfailing love! Both high and low among men find refuge in the shadow of your wings. Psalm 36:7

What a wonder—that God loves us so completely—so unconditionally. We don't have to *earn* His love—we just have to learn to *dwell* in His love. Awesome! We have a real-life Prince who has rescued us from death, hell and the grave—and He loves us! If no one else in the world loves us, who cares? Jesus loves me, this I know, for the Bible tells me so. Praise God!

Now, what kind of a royal romance would we have if we did not love God in return for all that He has done on our behalf? My guess is that there would not be a wedding, because He is a jealous God. In fact, He requires complete fidelity and faithfulness on the part of His bride. That is why He gave Moses this command and promise:

*"You shall not make for yourself an idol in the form of anything in heaven above or on the earth beneath or in the waters below. You shall not bow down to them or worship them; for I, the LORD your God, am a **jealous God**, punishing the children for the sin of the fathers to the third and fourth generation of those who hate me, but showing love to a thousand generations of those who love me and keep my commandments. Exodus 20:4-6*

Have you ever been to church with a bunch of lukewarm Christians? During praise and worship, they barely sing, clap, raise their hands, or do anything that would indicate that they are in love with Jesus. I hope this doesn't describe you. Anyway, I guess there are different degrees of love when it comes to loving God, because Jesus told a parable to some religious leaders who thought they were too important to show affection to Jesus. He told them this story:

"Two men owed money to a certain moneylender. One owed him five hundred denarii, and the other fifty. Neither of them had the money to pay him back, so he canceled the debts of both. Now which of them will love him more?" Simon replied, "I suppose the one who had the bigger debt canceled." "You have judged correctly," Jesus said. Luke 7:41-43

Then he turned toward the woman and said to Simon, "Do you see this woman? I came into your house. You did not give me any water for my feet, but she wet my feet with tears and wiped them with her hair. You did not give me a kiss, but this woman, from the time I entered, has not stopped kissing my feet. You did not put oil on my head, but she has poured perfume on my feet. Therefore, I tell you, her many sins have been forgiven-for she loved much. But he who has been forgiven little loves little." Luke 7:44-47

I don't know about you, but I love affection. I am affectionate towards my husband, my children, my grandchildren, my friends, people at work, people at church, you name it, I am affectionate. Now, there are some things that I do to show affection for my husband that I don't do to other people—like kiss his earlobe. I would never do that to someone at church or at work—but I love doing it to my husband, and he likes it. My boys love it when I rub their heads and backs while lying on the couch, and most everyone else enjoys getting a hug occasionally, especially after a long absence.

I wonder how Jesus feels about affection. I'm pretty sure that he loves hearing us shout His praises, because there are scriptures to that effect. There are also commands to make a joyful noise unto the Lord, clap your hands all ye people, shout for joy unto the Lord, sing unto the Lord a new song, dance with the tambourine, blow the trumpet in Zion, etc. The scriptures are too numerous to mention, so you can look them up if you want to. So, I wonder why so many churches seem more like museums than a praise party for Jesus. Is it because our love for Him has grown cold? Would you be willing to kiss the feet of Jesus as an act of affection and adoration, or are you a member of the church of Ephesus?

"To the angel of the church in Ephesus write: These are the words of him who holds the seven stars in his right hand and walks among the seven golden lampstands: I know your deeds, your hard work and your perseverance. I know that you cannot tolerate wicked men, that you have tested those who claim to be apostles but are not, and have found them false. You have persevered and have endured hardships for my name and have not grown weary. Revelation 2:1-3

Yet I hold this against you: You have forsaken your first love. Remember the height from which you have fallen! Repent and do the things you did at first. If you do not repent, I will come to you and remove your lampstand from its place. Revelation 2:4,5

If you look at the church at Ephesus, you can see that they were Christians who were hard at work doing good deeds. They had suffered persecution and defended the Gospel from false teachers. They were correct in their doctrine, and yet, they had forsaken their first love. God considers this sin, because He tells them to repent and do the things they did at first. Do you wonder why God would be so offended by these "good Christians"?

Just look at marriage, because it is a picture of our relationship with God. Before a couple is married, they are starry-eyed and in love. They are passionate about each other and want to be together all of the time. They go out to eat alone, sit at the table and talk to each other for hours. As newlyweds, my husband and I would sit for hours in the bathtub just to be together. Those were times forgetting to know each other better—times when the world and all of its problems seemed miles away.

Then, things begin to change. Husbands and wives get wrapped up in the daily stresses of going to work, doing chores, mowing the lawn, going shopping, paying bills, taking care of children, hanging out with friends, watching television, getting involved in sports. The list of distractions is unlimited, but you get the picture. We begin to take each other for granted and leave no time for romance, that's the time spent alone growing to love each other even more. Instead, the flame of passion dies down to an ember, and romantic love dies, leaving a dry, parched marriage devoid of life. A healthy marriage requires romantic love, an outflow of the agape love of God.

Let's face it, marriage without romance is a bore.

Our relationship with God is the same way. We may begin to take Him and His presence for granted. We may mature as children of God and become involved in all kinds of good works. We can become so busy doing good deeds that we fail to leave time for Him. Our hearts can grow cold, and we can forsake our first love. Don't let that happen! Our royal romance with the Prince of Peace requires time alone in worship—that place of intimacy in the very throne room of God, where we can touch the face of Jesus. God is romantic and affectionate. He wants us to be close enough to Him that we might **kiss the Son** *(Jesus)*, for it is in intimacy with Him that we are kept from evil.

Kiss the Son, *lest he be angry and you be destroyed in your way, for his wrath can flare up in a moment. Blessed are all who take refuge in him. Psalm 2:12*

It is not enough that we love God in return for all that He has done for us. This royal romance goes a step further. The apostle John, in his first letter to the churches, tells us about this divine love relationship.

We love because he first loved us. If anyone says, "I love God," yet hates his brother, he is a liar. For anyone who does not love his brother, whom he has seen, cannot love God, whom he has not seen. And he has given us this command: Whoever loves God must also love his brother. 1 John 4:19-21

Jesus also tells us that we must love others as ourselves.

Jesus replied: " `Love the Lord your God with all your heart and with all your soul and with all your mind.' This is the first and greatest commandment. And the second is like it: `Love your neighbor as yourself.' All the Law and the Prophets hang on these two commandments." Matthew 22:37-40

Jesus makes it clear that you cannot love God without loving other people, because each of the Ten Commandments is fulfilled in love. God wants to shed His agape *(unconditional)* love to others, and He does this through His obedient children. His desire is that we break the curse of evil over the lives of others, especially those who have done evil towards us. That is why we are commanded to love everyone, including anyone who has ever hurt us in any way. Jesus made this clear in His sermon on the mount:

"You have heard that it was said, `Love your neighbor and hate your enemy.' But I tell you: Love your enemies and pray for those who persecute you, that you may be sons of your Father in heaven. He causes his sun to rise on the evil and the good, and sends rain on the righteous and the unrighteous. If you love those who love you, what reward will you get? Are not even the tax collectors doing that? And if you greet only your brothers, what are you doing more than others? Do not even pagans do that? Be perfect, therefore, as your heavenly Father is perfect. Matthew 5:43-48

The apostle John, in his first letter to the churches, makes it clear that love is a requirement for royal service in the King's court.

This is how we know who the children of God are and who the children of the devil are: Anyone who does not do what is right is not a child of God; nor is anyone who does not love his brother. 1 John 3:10

> *The only evidence that will stand up in the high court of Heaven. to validate a person's Christianity is agape love— the ability and willingness to love others, including our enemies.*

Non-Christians—pagans, those who worship idols, those who practice witchcraft, Muslims, Hindus, and others who do not know Christ—generally love their own family members to a degree. Only a committed Christian, one who has submitted his heart and will to Jesus, can love an enemy.

God is the same yesterday, today, and tomorrow. That is why He has not changed His mind since He wrote the book of Leviticus in the Old Testament. He told the Israelites then, and it still applies to us today:

Do not seek revenge or bear a grudge against one of your people but love your neighbor as yourself. I am the LORD. Leviticus 19:18

The apostle Peter, in his first letter to the churches, tells us that we must love one another deeply, from the heart.

Now that you have purified yourselves by obeying the truth so that you have sincere love for your brothers, love one another deeply, from the heart. 1 Peter 1:22

Paul, in his letter to the Romans gave us clear instructions on how we are to love God and others. He said:

Love must be sincere. Hate what is evil; cling to what is good. Be devoted to one another in brotherly love. Honor one another above yourselves. Never be lacking in zeal, but keep your spiritual fervor, serving the Lord. Be joyful in hope, patient in affliction, faithful in prayer. Share with God's people who are in need. Practice hospitality. Romans 12:9-13

Now, that is a mouthful. Love must be sincere—not fake or fabricated. Love that does not flow from the heart of God is no love at all. Love hates what is evil, because it destroys lives. Love clings to what is good, because love always wants what is best for others.

Paul also tells us that we are to be devoted to one another in brotherly love. Have you ever thought about what this means?

Webster says…

Devotion:
- *A strong attachment or affection to a person or cause;*
- *Zeal;*
- *To apply time completely to some activity;*
- *To concentrate on time or energy;*

That is what I call commitment. We are to be committed to the well-being of others, especially those within the Body of Christ. This is love, the kind of love that compels us to share with others who are in need and also practice hospitality. Now, that's a rare commodity these days. We schedule ourselves so heavily with sports, hobbies, and after work activities that very few Christians leave time for hospitality. Without hospitality, how do we grow in our relationships with other Christians? We don't. When you get right down to it, maybe we need to deny ourselves enough distractions —activities that consume our time, money, and attention—to allow time for others who may just need a friend. The apostle John tells us what sincere love looks like.

This is how we know what love is: Jesus Christ laid down his life for us. And we ought to lay down our lives for our brothers. If anyone has material possessions and sees his brother in need but has no pity on him, how can the love of God be in him? Dear children, let us not love with words or tongue but with actions and in truth. 1 John 3:16-18

Simon Peter was a fisherman by trade. He and his brother had a little business down by the Sea of Galilee, and if you went looking for him, you would probably find him on his boat or repairing one of his nets. One day after eating some fish, Jesus asked Simon Peter if he really loved Him—more than his fish, his boats, his nets, his career, his way of life.

"Simon son of John, do you truly love me more than these?" "Yes, Lord," he said, "you know that I love you." Jesus said, "Feed my lambs." Again, Jesus said, "Simon son of John, do you truly love me?" He answered, "Yes, Lord, you know that I love you." Jesus said, "Take care of my sheep." The third time he said to him, "Simon son of John, do you love me?" Peter was hurt because Jesus asked him the third time, "Do you love me?" He said, "Lord, you know all things; you know that I love you." Jesus said, "Feed my sheep." John 21:15-17

Jesus also told Peter what kind of death he would die—crucifixion— and said, *"Follow me."* Jesus asks the same question of you, *"Do you really love me? Are you willing to follow in My footsteps and walk the way of the cross?"* Jesus says to those whose hearts are willing:

"As the Father has loved me, so have I loved you. Now remain in my love. If you obey my commands, you will remain in my love, just as I have obeyed my Father's commands and remain in his love. I have told you this so that my joy may be in you and that your joy may be complete. My command is this: Love each other as I have loved you. John 15:9

Points to Ponder...

- Are you willing to make changes necessary in your life so that you may be useful for His purposes?
- Are you willing to take up your cross, die to your own agenda, repent of known sins, and follow Jesus?
- Are you willing to forgive everyone for anything they may have done to hurt you?
- Are you willing to love the unlovely?
- Are you willing to free up your schedule so that there is time in it to meet the needs of others?
- Do you really love others as yourself?

Quiet Time...

Dearest Heavenly Father,

I confess that, at times, I have taken our relationship for granted and have not made time in my schedule for intimacy with You. I have filled my life with so much activity, that I have little time for You or for anyone else, for that matter. Please forgive me and embrace me with Your unfailing love. Pour out Your Spirit upon me and anoint me for service in your royal courts. Show me the way to Your heart so that I might lead others into the saving knowledge of Jesus Christ. Open the doors of opportunity so that I might serve Your people. I love you, Lord. I am Yours, and You are forever mine. *Amen.*

Be imitators of God, therefore,
as dearly loved children and live a life of love,
just as Christ loved us and gave himself up for us as a fragrant offering and sacrifice
to God.
Ephesians 5:1,2

CHAPTER 13

The *Merciful Servant*

Remember, O LORD, your great mercy and love, for they are from old. Remember not the sins of my youth and my rebellious ways; according to your love remember me, for you are good, O LORD. Psalm 25:6,7

Regardless of who you are, your education or status in life, God is calling you into full-time ministry as a royal servant in the King's court. Does that mean that you are to leave your profession, go to seminary and become a pastor or missionary in Africa? Probably not. The fact is that every child of God is called into full-time ministry at home, at work and at play. He might even use you at church, but don't wait for that door to open before you become a servant. He simply wants you to serve others as the need arises right where you live. We are all called to be ambassadors for Christ, to be His hands, feet, and mouthpiece for those who need a touch from the Master's hand.

One of the greatest qualifications for royal service in the King's court is *mercy*. God's *love and mercy* are two sides of the same coin. A person who has God's agape love is merciful. A person who is not merciful does not have God's love— and that person does not qualify for service in the King's court.

What is mercy anyway? Let us look at this word from God's point of view. First of all, the Bible says that God is *merciful.* You see, we have all sinned against Him and fallen short of the glory of God. Each of us deserves death and the wrath of God, but instead, in His mercy, He sent Jesus Christ to die for our sins. Instead of the death that we so deserve, His *mercy* offers us eternal life! That is *mercy*.

Who is a God like you, who pardons sin and forgives the transgression of the remnant of his inheritance? You do not stay angry forever but delight to show mercy. Micah 7:18

> *Webster says…*
>
> *Mercy:*
> - *Kindness and forgiveness, especially when given to a person who does not deserve it;*
> - *Compassionate and kind treatment;*

Two scriptures give us a clear indication of how God feels about mercy in the lives of His children. First of all, God is more interested in mercy than religious activity. Many Christians feel secure that they are about the Father's business because they may preach in the pulpit, teach Sunday school, or sing in the choir. They may go to church every time the doors are open, tithe, and carry their Bibles to work. Is this what God really desires? Let us see.

*For I **desire mercy**, not sacrifice, and acknowledgment of God rather than burnt offerings. Hosea 6:6*

> **Power Principle #39**
> *God not only **desires** mercy, but He also **requires** mercy.*

*He has showed you, O man, what is good. And what does the LORD **require** of you? To act justly and to **love mercy** and to walk humbly with your God. Micah 6:8*

Basically, of the three things God **requires** of us, **mercy** is at the center of His heart. If we dissect this scripture, we can see why. First of all, we are required to act justly—which means that we live our lives in obedience to His commands motivated by His love. We are also required to live out our daily lives in humble submission to God's will, enjoying His presence. Humility is a character trait that allows us to see our own sin and our incredible need for a savior. Humility understands that, apart from the **mercy** of God, we would burn in hell for eternity. Humility is grateful for the saving power of the blood of Jesus. Humility says of another person, *"There, but by the grace of God, go I."*

> *Mercy is the glow of God's love in a humble heart.*

King David was called a man after God's own heart. Yes, he was human and failed miserably in many ways. After all, he committed adultery with another man's wife and then plotted the man's murder in order to cover up his sin. On another occasion, he became puffed up with pride over the size of his army and ordered that a census be taken against the will of God. He completely failed as a father and leader of God's people, when his oldest son, Amnon, molested his beautiful daughter, Tamar. He even failed to deal justly with his son, Absalom, after he took revenge and murdered Amnon for raping his sister. In spite of all his sins and shortcomings as a king, friend, and father, he never lost touch with his God. From the depths of his soul, David cried out to God for **mercy.**

*I said, "O LORD, have **mercy** on me; heal me, for I have sinned against you." Psalm 41:4*

David was acutely aware that all of his unrighteous acts were acts of rebellion against God. He committed adultery with the wife of a dear friend, Uriah the Hittite, but he sinned against God by breaking the commandment prohibiting the act of adultery. He murdered Uriah the Hittite, but he sinned against God by breaking the commandment prohibiting murder. He failed to deal with his son, Amnon, after he raped Absalom's sister Tamar, in accordance with the Law of Moses. He broke the first and second commandments of God when he ordered the census of his men— because for that moment in time, David placed himself in the seat of honor within his own heart. That is why, when he felt the heavy guilt of sin upon his life, he cried out again:

*Have **mercy** on me, O God, according to your unfailing love; according to your great compassion blot out my transgressions. Wash away all my iniquity and cleanse me from my sin. For I know my transgressions, and my sin is always before me. Psalm 51:1*

This is the place I found myself in 1980, when I came to my senses, turned from my sinful lifestyle and ran to the merciful and compassionate arms of a loving God. He had never left me nor forsaken me but waited patiently for me to see the error of my ways. It only took a bad marriage, divorce, losing custody of my precious son, my home and all of my belongings—and, more importantly, losing all sense of morality and self-respect—to realize that locked inside a spiritual pigpen is the last place I want to be. God, in His loving compassion and mercy, allowed me to descend deep into the darkest caverns of depression and the edge of suicide—all the while waiting for me to surrender myself to His loving presence.

Anyone who has ever experienced the incredible mercy of God in their lives—the kind of mercy that brings forth eternal life from the ashes of a broken heart—cannot help but cry out in humility:

*Praise be to the LORD, for he has heard my cry for **mercy**. Psalm 28:6*

To whom much has been given, much is expected. If we have received mercy from God, how much more are we expected to give mercy to those who need it? Many in the church still struggle with extending mercy, especially to those who are bound up in sinful lifestyles.

Things have not changed over the last 2,000 years—religious self-righteous people will generally "look down their noses" at those who have yet to find freedom from sinful lifestyles. Consider the time Jesus was having dinner at Matthew's house. Remember him? He was a tax collector for the Roman government. Most tax collectors were corrupt, taking more from the people than was required by law and keeping the excess for themselves—sounds like some of our own government officials. Anyway, while they were eating, many tax collectors and "sinners" came and joined them for dinner. Apparently, some Pharisees *(religious leaders)* were snooping around as they usually did to spy on Jesus, when they asked his disciples:

---

*"Why does your teacher eat with tax collectors and `sinners'?"* *On hearing this, Jesus said, "It is not the healthy who need a doctor, but the sick. But go and learn what this means: `I desire **mercy**, not sacrifice.' For I have not come to call the righteous, but sinners." Matthew 9:11-13*

As the recipients of God's great **mercy**, we have an obligation to forgive those who have offended us. It does not matter how small or how great the offense may have been, it must be forgiven. Were you molested or physically abused as a child? Perhaps you were abandoned by your father or mother. Were your parents alcoholics or drug addicts, and neglectful of their parental responsibilities? Maybe your husband or wife has left you for someone else. Did a sibling rob you of your inheritance? Have you been falsely accused of a crime? Have you been embezzled or robbed by a trusted friend or family member? Have you been overlooked for promotion at work time and again? Have you been betrayed by those you love? Have you been abandoned by family or friends during your time of greatest need? If so, you must forgive, deeply from the heart, for you reap what you sow. This is why Jesus said in His great Sermon on the Mount:

*"Blessed are the **merciful**, for they will be shown **mercy**". Matthew 5:7*

I learned this lesson early in life, when my best friend betrayed me and broke my heart. When I came home crying from school that Friday afternoon, my wise and compassionate mother told me that I must forgive her and pray for her, which I did. Two days later, on Sunday afternoon, my girlfriend called me crying and asked me to forgive her. That was a lesson well learned—one that I'll never forget.

My husband and I have had many opportunities to extend **mercy** throughout the 25 years of our marriage. First of all, we have had to forgive each other. We came into our marriage with a truckload of emotional baggage. We were both easily offended during the early years of our marriage, until God began to heal our broken hearts. **Forgiveness paved the way for healing**, and we now have a marriage that is just this side of heaven.

We also had to forgive a family member who embezzled over $200,000 from our small company, while we went without paychecks. We had to forgive her for falsely accusing us of Medicare fraud in order to receive immunity for her crime. We had to forgive her for slandering our name and causing us to suffer through four years of a grand jury investigation. *Forgiveness paved the way for God's deliverance*, and we walked through the fire victoriously.

We had to forgive "friends" who walked out of our life when the F.B.I. walked in to do their investigation. Abandoned by many who proclaimed to be Christians, our grief knew no boundaries. When we needed the comfort and prayers of those we loved, we instead received the "friends of Job". *Forgiveness paved the way for God's comforting presence,* and we found the "peace that passes all understanding" in the midst of our storm.

We had to forgive Christians who held leadership positions in our company, when they walked away with over $2,000,000 worth of business in a mass betrayal of confidence and friendship. *Forgiveness paved the way for God's provision,* and He has restored to us seven times what was stolen.

We have had the opportunity to forgive other friends who embezzled from our company; employees who have sued us for every conceivable reason; people who misjudge us—the list is unending. *Forgiveness paved the way for God's protection,* and no weapon formed against us by man has prospered.

Power Principle #40
*The seeds of **mercy** produce forgiveness and a crop of blessing.*

Mercy comes in different packages. When we showed *mercy* towards those who sought to do us harm, we forgave those who trespassed against us. We harvested a crop of blessing as God healed our broken hearts, comforted us in our time of distress, delivered us from the evil one, and gave us peace of mind and heart.

Because we praised God and prayed for those who misused us, we prospered spiritually and financially in the midst of our circumstances. Praise God for His unfailing love!

Jesus certainly understood the need to forgive—*forgiveness paved the way to the cross.* It was through forgiveness that sinful men and women could be restored to a life-giving relationship with our heavenly Father. ***Forgiveness paved the way from death to life!***

Jesus told His disciples that the kingdom of heaven is like a king who wanted to settle some accounts owed by his servants. One man owed him a ton of money. When he could not pay up, the king ordered that he, along with his wife and children, be sold as slaves to repay the debt. When the servant fell on his knees and begged for mercy, the king took pity on him, canceled the debt, and let him go.

Obviously, this fellow wasn't very smart, because he immediately found one of his neighbors who owed him a couple of dollars. He grabbed him by the throat and demanded that he pay back what he owed. When the poor man fell on his knees and begged him for mercy, the evil servant had him thrown into prison.

You know, the eyes of the Lord are everywhere. Apparently, some other servants of the king saw the whole thing and were very upset. So, they went and told the king everything they had seen. The king was very angry and called the evil servant back to the palace, and this is what he said:

*'You wicked servant,' he said, `I canceled all that debt of yours because you begged me to. Shouldn't you have had **mercy** on your fellow servant just as I had on you?' In anger his master turned him over to the jailers to be tortured, until he should pay back all he owed. "This is how my heavenly Father will treat each of you unless you forgive your brother from your heart." Matthew 18:32-35*

There is hardly a Christian who has not heard this parable of Jesus concerning forgiveness; yet why is there so much bitterness in the hearts of God's people? Why is there so much divorce within the church? Why are there so many broken relationships among God's people? Perhaps there is personal pride laced with a lack of mercy.

A friend of mine has struggled for years to remain in a marriage to a man who does not love her. He has abandoned her emotionally and sexually, and they live single lives within the same house. Why is he harsh with her? Why can't he love her the way Christ loves the church, even though he is a Bible-believing Christian? *Mercy* looks beyond the offense to the brokenness that has never received the healing touch of the Great Physician. In this case, when this husband was a young man, his mother committed suicide; years later, his stepmother committed suicide. How deep is the stronghold of abandonment and rejection in the heart of this man? Mercy looks at a harsh, unloving husband and says, "Father, forgive him, for he does not know what he is doing." *Mercy* seeks to understand the root cause of sin and offers unconditional love in the place of judgment.

As children of God, we are called and required to show forth *mercy* to others— especially to those within our own families and churches. James gives a warning to the people of God:

*Speak and act as those who are going to be judged by the law that gives freedom, because judgment without **mercy** will be shown to anyone who has not been **merciful**. Mercy triumphs over judgment! James 2:12*

Judgment without *mercy* will be shown to anyone who has not been merciful.

Power Principle #41
Forgiveness is available for those who forgive.

That is why, when Jesus taught His disciples how to pray, he included this in His prayer:

Forgive us for our debts, as we also have forgiven our debtors. Matthew 6:12

Jesus went on to say:

For if you forgive men when they sin against you, your heavenly Father will also forgive you. But if you do not forgive men their sins, your Father will not forgive your sins. Matthew 6:14,15

The Old Testament prophet Zechariah spoke the word of the LORD when he said:

This is what the LORD Almighty says: `Administer true justice; show mercy and compassion to one another. Do not oppress the widow or the fatherless, the alien or the poor. In your hearts do not think evil of each other.' Zechariah 7:9,10

> *God's unconditional love within a **merciful** and **humble** heart— qualifications for royal service in the King's court.*

The royal servant is prepared to draw the lost, the lonely, and the destitute towards a loving Father, who patiently waits for the prodigal to come home. With this in mind, remember:

*Be **merciful** to those who doubt; snatch others from the fire and save them; to others show **mercy**, mixed with fear-hating even the clothing stained by corrupted flesh. Jude 1:22,23*

Points to Ponder...

- Are you easily offended? If so, have you ever wondered why?
- Have you ever been the victim of abuse or molestation? If so, have you sought healing for these wounds through forgiveness, prayer and Christian counseling?
- How hard is it for you to forgive offenses? Are you willing to pray for those who have hurt you?
- Are you willing to allow God to remove all bitterness from your heart?
- Do you easily find fault with others?
- Are you compassionate towards those in need? Do you offer to help in some way?
- When was the last time you gave of your time and attention to comfort someone else?

Quiet Time...

Dearest Heavenly Father,

Thank you for Your mercies that are new every morning. No matter how bad I did yesterday, I can choose to do better today. I confess that I have fallen for Satan's trap and hurt those I should love the most—members of my own family. In addition, I sometimes find it difficult to forgive those who have offended me.
Instead of praying for my enemies, I choose to hold on to the offenses that choke Your life right out of my heart. Please forgive me, Lord, as I choose to forgive others. Help me to cultivate a heart of mercy towards everyone. I love You, Lord.
I am Yours, and You are forever mine. *Amen.*

Turn to me and have mercy on me, as you always do to those who love your name. Direct my footsteps according to your word; let no sin rule over me.
Psalm 119:132,133

CHAPTER 14

The *Crown*

Blessed is the man who perseveres under trial, because when he has stood the test, he will receive the crown of life that God has promised to those who love him. JAS 1:12

Coronation Day—an event to remember—a day of thrilling excitement as throngs gather to see the appointed heir receive the crown that has long awaited his coming of age!

The royal procession has left the palace; horses and carriages adorned in jewels and covered in roses, traveling to the cadence of trumpets and drums through expectant crowds of adoring admirers. Can you imagine yourself stretching to see over the crowds, just to get a glimpse of the soon-to-be king? People are pushing and shoving to get closer to the place where he will pass by. Such anticipation, as the crowd presses in to see if he might be coming around the bend in the road. The noise is exhilarating as the people cheer at the sight of the royal caravan making the turn towards the great cathedral. Oh, to be one invited to the actual ceremony—what a longing in the hearts of the common people to be a part of the royal celebration to follow. *Imagine.*

Imagine that you have been invited to witness the crowning of the Prince within the walls of the magnificent cathedral. As you enter the cavernous sanctuary, your heart is filled with awe at the splendor of these unfamiliar surroundings. You notice that the high ceilings, gilded in gold with paintings that reflect the glory of God, seem to open up to the radiance of heaven. Light filters through the enormous painted glass windows, each telling a story of faith and courage from long, long ago. Flickering candles line the stone walls of the massive building, each a warm reminder of the One Who is light and His power to overcome darkness. The beauty and fragrance of tens of thousands of flowers—roses of every color and variety, and lilies of the valley, tulips, dahlias, white, pink, and lavender callas, hydrangeas, geraniums, and too many others to mention—capture your senses, carrying you to a place in the Spirit where man once walked with God.

The sounds of trumpets and other wind instruments, strings, percussion and a thousand voices begin to resound in heavenly harmony, and you begin to sense the holy presence of a greater King. You take notice of the invited guests—too numerous to count—each dressed for the royal occasion in velvets and satins, with threads of glittering gold reflecting the light of a thousand candles. The sights, sounds and fragrances bring you to a different sanctuary, where thousands and thousands of angels cry, *"Holy, holy, holy, is the LORD God Almighty, Who was, and is, and Who is to come!"* And suddenly—it happens!

The room grows quiet as the musicians and singers rise to their feet. The trumpets are sounded! Outside, the crowds fall to their knees as the Prince ascends the steps toward his destiny. The massive doors open as hundreds of trumpets proclaim his entry. Inside, the people stand and watch in wonder as the royal procession passes by. *Imagine.*

The ceremony begins. The musicians and singers burst forth in glorious songs of thanksgiving and praise until every heart has felt the finger of God. Prayers are offered up to the greater King, and finally, it is time. The crown—oh, the crown! How awesome and glorious it is, made of pure gold—free from all corruption— you can almost see through it. The jewels—diamonds, rubies, sapphires, topaz, emeralds, pearls, stones of every color, some you have never seen before—have a light of their own, it seems. The brilliance from each stone creates a halo of color as the crown is held above the uplifted face of the prince. *Imagine. Just imagine.*

Whose face is that? Imagine that it is yours! *Just imagine!* The cheers of throngs of people surround you as your knees give way, and you are kissing the feet of your great High Priest. Could this be true? How is this possible? You are lost in worship—for how long, you cannot know—until you are carried on the wings of a great Eagle to the royal residence of the Greater King.

The celebration continues at the magnificent banquet hall in the glorious mansion prepared for you before the beginning of time. It is too much to comprehend, for the beauty and splendor found here far surpasses anything the human mind can grasp. The guests also arrive, and it appears that all are clothed in royal splendor with a halo of color, a glow resting on each face. A royal feast has been prepared, and the celebration continues with laughter, love, and unspeakable joy—for how long? *Imagine. A place where time does not exist—a place of unending joy— imagine.*

Power Principle #42
A proper vision of eternity transforms the human heart.

Why would anyone be willing to give up the riches of this world—fame and fortune —to serve others? Who can blame the "rich young ruler"—the one spoken about in the book of Matthew—for refusing Jesus' offer of eternal life? He must have been standing around in the crowd listening to Jesus teach, when he asked,

"Teacher, what good thing must I do to get eternal life?" "Why do you ask me about what is good?" Jesus replied. "There is only One who is good. If you want to enter life, obey the commandments." "Which ones?" the man inquired. Jesus replied, " `Do not murder, do not commit adultery, do not steal, do not give false testimony, honor your father and mother,' and `love your neighbor as yourself.'" Matthew 19:16-19

"All these I have kept," the young man said. "What do I still lack?" Jesus answered, "If you want to be perfect, go, sell your possessions and give to the poor, and you will have treasure in heaven. Then come, follow me." When the young man heard this, he went away sad, because he had great wealth. Matthew 19:20-22

It is obvious from this story that the young man was very interested in getting to heaven and escaping hell. After all, he was a religious and moral young man, since he confessed to Jesus that he had kept all of the requirements of the law. However, he was very aware that something else was missing—that is why he asked, *"What do I still lack?"*

The fact is, religion will get you nowhere with God, and it will always leave you empty, unfulfilled, and spiritually destitute. This young man is so typical of rich Americans—and in case you don't know it yet, compared to the rest of humanity, all Americans are rich. He is typical, because he was a slave to his possessions, his possessions owned him, and he was unwilling to walk away from his wealth in order to obtain eternal life. That is why Jesus turned to His disciples and said,

"I tell you the truth, it is hard for a rich man to enter the kingdom of heaven. Again, I tell you, it is easier for a camel to go through the eye of a needle than for a rich man to enter the kingdom of God." Matthew 19:23,24

Two thousand years later, the rich young ruler no longer walks upon the earth. Wherever he is spending his eternity, he exited this earth without his riches, they were left behind for someone else to enjoy. We will all go the way of this young man one day. Each of us will face our eternal destiny, and when we do, we will leave this earth the same way we came into the world—naked and penniless. So, why do we Christians have such a hard time saying yes to God? Why are so many in the church chasing after the riches of this world, rather than the greater riches of His eternal kingdom? Is it because we cannot *imagine* how glorious our inheritance will be? Are we so earthly minded that we cannot fathom the riches of God's eternal kingdom?

Our little story at the beginning of this chapter is not far from the truth. Because I have not personally physically visited heaven, I cannot give a completely accurate picture of all that awaits us; but I can assure you, it is better than I portrayed. If we could get just one tiny glimpse of what the apostle John saw in his visions, as recorded in the book of Revelation, we would never live our lives for the pleasures of this life.

Power Principle #43
One tiny glimpse of the glory of God will change the way you live.

Since the beginning of time, God has been trying to tell us about His kingdom and all the blessings that await a child of God. He sent his prophets of the Old Testament to proclaim the truth of His eternal love and riches that will never rot nor rust—riches that will last forever. When the fullness of time came, He even sent Jesus Christ, His only begotten Son, to proclaim His kingdom to those who would listen. Can you imagine all of the people who actually sat in the presence of Jesus, heard him teach and preach, and yet, turned back to do their own thing? How many of those poor souls—people who had the law and the prophets, went to the temple on feast days, did all of the religious stuff that Jewish people did back then—regret that they made the same decision as the rich young ruler? Only God knows, and it grieves Him. That is why Jesus said,

"No one who puts his hand to the plow and looks back is fit for service in the kingdom of God." Luke 9:62

Does this warning from the mouth of Jesus mean anything to you? It should remind you of a woman who lived and died during Abraham's time on earth. She was the wife of Abraham's nephew Lot, who had chosen to leave his righteous uncle to live among the most pagan, sin-filled city in the land of promise— Sodom—all for the **love of money**.

If you remember the story, God had his fill of sin from those wicked people, so he warned Abraham of the coming destruction of Sodom and Gomorrah. After some serious negotiations between the Lord and Abraham, God sent two angels to get Lot and his family out of town before it was too late. The angels had to practically drag Lot, his wife, and two daughters out of the city. When they were a distance away, Lot's wife looked back towards the city and the home that she loved. She looked back and partook of the wrath of God—she became a pillar of salt. She died. She did not live. Lot left the blessings of God's promise for the wealth of this world. Like the rich young ruler who walked away from his divine destiny, Lot died a penniless, hopeless failure as a husband and father.

> *Lot chose the riches of this world rather than the promise of God and lost his eternal inheritance.*

Why would any sane person choose to serve others and forsake all that the world offers? First and foremost, we do it because we love God. We do His will because we love Him and want to please him. Jesus said,

"If anyone loves me, he will obey my teaching. My Father will love him, and we will come to him and make our home with him. He who does not love me will not obey my teaching." John 14:23,24

Because we love God, He comes and makes His home in our hearts. He creates in us a new heart, one that is free from sin—free from unnecessary matter, such as unforgiveness, bitterness, greed, envy, hatred, anger, anxiety and fear—and He fills us with His unconditional love for others. Because we love others, we willingly lay down our own agenda to serve those who are in need. We become partakers of the divine nature of God.

The Gospel of Jesus Christ is great news! Jesus died so that we could be *free from sin* and *free to obey* God's royal law of love. As we live to please Him and do His will, He opens our spiritual eyes to see a little glimpse of heaven and the promised inheritance that is stored up for those who love Him. He also opens our hearts to *wisdom* and to *understand* the glory that awaits a faithful child of God. For instance, Proverbs tells us:

***Wisdom** is supreme; therefore, get **wisdom**. Though it costs all you have, get **understanding**. Esteem her, and she will exalt you; embrace her, and she will honor you. She will set a garland of grace on your head and present you with a **crown of splendor**." Proverbs 4:7-9*

Wisdom is the ability to use knowledge in a way that is pleasing to God. As you seek to understand from the heart, you will be easily led by God to do His will. As you are obedient to His will, His blessings will overtake your life, and you will be more than victorious in your daily life. Proverbs tell us that blessings will *crown* the head of those who do the will of God.

*Blessings **crown** the head of the righteous, but violence overwhelms the mouth of the wicked. Proverbs 10:6*

God's word promises that blessings—not curses—will cover your head like a ***garland***: symbolic of the ***garland*** that was once placed upon the heads of conquering heroes upon their return from the battle. You can become a victorious conqueror for God's kingdom on Earth, setting those captives to the evil one free to know, love and serve God. One day, you will receive a ***crown of splendor***— symbolic of leadership in God's eternal kingdom.

When we live our lives according to the will of God in order to please Him, we walk in the footsteps of Jesus. That is why He told us to take up our cross and follow Him. We must do what Jesus did. What was His job description? Jesus quoted Isaiah and applied this prophesy to Himself:

*The Spirit of the Sovereign LORD is on me, because the LORD has anointed me to preach good news to the poor. He has sent me to bind up the brokenhearted, to proclaim freedom for the captives and release from darkness for the prisoners, to proclaim the year of the LORD's favor and the day of vengeance of our God, to comfort all who mourn, and provide for those who grieve in Zion—to bestow on them a **crown of beauty** instead of ashes, the oil of gladness instead of mourning, and a garment of praise instead of a spirit of despair. They will be called oaks of righteousness, a planting of the LORD for the display of his splendor. Isaiah 61:1-3*

This is what Jesus did for you and for me and for every other lost lamb that has ever heard His voice and responded with a grateful heart. He called out to me in my darkest hour. He called me! The Creator of the universe heard my cry for help, and He called me to Himself. He took me into His loving care and healed my broken heart. He set me free from sin and released me from my prison of depression and hopelessness. He forgave me for my sinful ways, comforted me in my trials, provided for me in times of need, and *crowned me with beauty instead of ashes*. He filled my life with joy and gladness instead of mourning, and replaced my despair with a garment of praise. I am a new creation. The old Connie, the one who lived a life in rebellion against God, is gone. I am a new woman—a woman of noble character—no longer a twig tossed around by the storms of life, but rather a solid oak of righteousness, a planting of the LORD for the display of *HIS splendor*. He did it all!

Jesus left the splendor of His Father's presence and the glorious praises of hosts of angels that worshipped Him night and day in order to find me, save me, and change me. He did it for you and for every human being that has ever lived. He gave up the *crown of heaven* and took upon Himself a *crown of thorns*. Matthew tells us about this crown:

*Then the governor's soldiers took Jesus into the Praetorium and gathered the whole company of soldiers around him. They stripped him and put a scarlet robe on him, and then twisted together a **crown of thorns** and set it on his head. They put a staff in his right hand and knelt in front of him and mocked him. "Hail, king of the Jews!" they said. Matthew 27:27-29*

Imagine. Sinful men stripped the King of heaven, once clothed in glorious splendor, naked. They put a red robe on him and, placing a *crown of thorns* upon His head, mocked Him. He could have called down legions of angels to destroy the Roman soldiers and the entire city of Jerusalem. He could have simply spoken a word, and the planet would have been tossed into the sun like a beach ball. He did not do what you or I would have done, had we been vessels of the power of Almighty God. He simply obeyed His Father. Jesus won the prize that was set before Him. He found the pearl of great price—you and me—and he sold everything He had to purchase us. He fought the fight and won the battle. You are His prize, and He is your *crown of glory*.

*In that day the LORD Almighty will be a glorious **crown**, a beautiful wreath for the remnant of his people. ISA 28:5*

How do we win the prize? The same way that Jesus did. The apostle Paul tells us in his first letter to the church at Corinth:

*Do you not know that in a race all the runners run, but only one gets the prize? Run in such a way as to get the prize. Everyone who competes in the games goes into strict training. They do it to get **a crown that will not last**; but we do it to get **a crown that will last forever**. Therefore, I do not run like a man running aimlessly; I do not fight like a man beating the air. No, I beat my body and make it my slave so that after I have preached to others, I myself will not be disqualified for the prize. 1Corinthians 9:24-27*

Again, Paul tells Timothy in his second letter to this devout man of God:

*Endure hardship with us like a good soldier of Christ Jesus. No one serving as a soldier gets involved in civilian affairs--he wants to please his commanding officer. Similarly, if anyone competes as an athlete, he does not receive the **victor's crown** unless he competes according to the rules. 2Timothy 2:3-5*

Eternal rewards await the love-filled faithful servant of God. Whether you help an elderly widow with her grocery shopping, brush the teeth of an invalid, or comfort a hurting child—whatever you do—God is keeping track. Jesus told His disciples about that day of reckoning. He said:

"When the Son of Man comes in his glory, and all the angels with him, he will sit on his throne in heavenly glory. All the nations will be gathered before him, and he will separate the people one from another as a shepherd separates the sheep from the goats. He will put the sheep on his right and the goats on his left. Matthew 25:31-33

"Then the King will say to those on his right, `Come, you who are blessed by my Father, take your inheritance, the kingdom prepared for you since the creation of the world. For I was hungry and you gave me something to eat, I was thirsty and you gave me something to drink, I was a stranger and you invited me in, I needed clothes and you clothed me, I was sick and you looked after me, I was in prison and you came to visit me.' Matthew 25:34-36

"Then the righteous will answer him, `Lord, when did we see you hungry and feed you, or thirsty and give you something to drink? When did we see you a stranger and invite you in, or needing clothes and clothe you? When did we see you sick or in prison and go to visit you?" "The King will reply, `I tell you the truth, whatever you did for one of the least of these brothers of mine, you did for me.' Matthew 25:37-40

"Then he will say to those on his left, `Depart from me, you who are cursed, into the eternal fire prepared for the devil and his angels. For I was hungry and you gave me nothing to eat, I was thirsty and you gave me nothing to drink, I was a stranger and you did not invite me in, I needed clothes and you did not clothe me, I was sick and in prison and you did not look after me.' Matthew 25:41-43

"They also will answer, `Lord, when did we see you hungry or thirsty or a stranger or needing clothes or sick or in prison, and did not help you?" "He will reply, `I tell you the truth, whatever you did not do for one of the least of these, you did not do for me.' "Then they will go away to eternal punishment, but the righteous to eternal life." Matthew 25:44-46

You may notice that God did not say, "If you preach in the pulpit, sing in the choir, go to church every Sunday, read your Bible, or belong to a particular denomination, you inherit eternal life." **What is the mark of a heaven-bound child of God? Compassion that results in acts of mercy.**

Power Principle #44
Compassion *is the trademark of heaven—*
the key that gains entrance for the royal servant in the King's court.

To those who are called to lead God's people, the apostle Peter does have some instructions:

*To the elders among you, I appeal as a fellow elder, a witness of Christ's sufferings and one who also will share in the glory to be revealed: Be shepherds of God's flock that is under your care, serving as overseers--not because you must, but because you are willing, as God wants you to be; not greedy for money, but eager to serve; not lording it over those entrusted to you, but being examples to the flock. And when the Chief Shepherd appears, you will receive the **crown of glory** that will never fade away. 1 Peter 5:1-4*

A **crown of glory** awaits all who minister to the needs of others, no matter how great or small—a **crown** that will never ever fade or tarnish or lose its luster. The apostle Paul suffered greatly for the sake of God's people. While in prison awaiting his own execution, he wrote to his dear son in the Lord, Timothy:

*For I am already being poured out like a drink offering, and the time has come for my departure. I have fought the good fight, I have finished the race, I have kept the faith. Now there is in store for me the **crown of righteousness**, which the Lord, the righteous Judge, will award to me on that day--and not only to me, but also to all who have longed for his appearing.*
2 Timothy 4:6-8

Are you ready for His appearing? Have you been preparing for that great coronation day, the day when all of humanity, both the living and the dead, will see with their own eyes the **crowning event of the ages?** The stage is set, and an audience of millions who have gone before us—a great cloud of witnesses—cheers us on. Why?

God knows that it is tough being a Christian in a pagan nation. However, compared to China, North Korea, Malaysia, Indonesia, Sudan, Nigeria, Egypt, Saudi Arabia, Pakistan, India, and most of the third world, we Americans have no excuse. Our brothers and sisters in Christ suffer unbelievable persecution, even to the point of death. It could be that one day, we may face the same types of sufferings. Are you ready? If it is difficult for you to sacrifice your time, your finances, your attention, your affections, your ambitions, your way of life in order to minister to the needs of others, will you be ready to give up your life? Jesus, in His letter to the church at Smyrna, says:

These are the words of him who is the First and the Last, who died and came to life again. I know your afflictions and your poverty--yet you are rich! I know the slander of those who say they are Jews and are not but are a synagogue of Satan. Do not be afraid of what you are about to suffer. I tell you; the devil will put some of you in prison to test you, and you will suffer persecution for ten days. Be faithful, even to the point of death, and I will give you the **crown of life**. *Revelation 2:8-10*

Are you ready? *Allow Jesus Christ to transform you...* ***from rags to royalty?***

Points to Ponder...

- Do you see a need to change your priorities to allow more time for service?
- Do you want to serve or be served?
- Do you have ears to hear what Jesus is saying to the church today?
- Are you anxious for Jesus to return to rule on the earth?
- Are you ready to see Him face to face? Will you be excited or ashamed?
- Is your life characterized by traits of nobility?

Quiet Time...

Dearest Heavenly Father,

How great Thou art, oh Lord! Your plan of redemption and the love that You pour out on my life is beyond understanding. Lord, I ask for wisdom to govern my life in order to please You, and an understanding of Your ways. Give me a glimpse of Your kingdom, and a heaven-bound focus for my life. Help me to let go of earthly things and cling to that which is eternal. I love You, Lord. I am Yours, and You are forever mine. *Amen.*

I am coming soon.
*Hold on to what you have, so that no one will take your **crown**.*
Him who overcomes I will make a pillar in the temple of my God.
Never again will he leave it.
I will write on him the name of my God and the name of the city of my God, the new Jerusalem, which is coming down out of heaven from my God; and I will also write on him my new name.
He who has an ear, let him hear what the Spirit says to the churches.
Revelation 3:11-13

Epilogue

"Who then is the faithful and wise servant, whom the master has put in charge of the servants in his household to give them their food at the proper time? It will be good for that servant whose master finds him doing so when he returns. I tell you the truth, he will put him in charge of all his possessions. Matthew 24:45-47

Jesus once told His disciples that the greatest in the kingdom is a servant to all. Obviously, Jesus is the greatest in the kingdom, since He alone became a suffering servant for all of mankind—past, present, and all those who have yet to be born. He gave all that he had, so that we could become all that He is. This is our commission. This is what pleases God and brings Him glory and honor on the earth—to become royal servants for the King—doing His bidding, shedding His love and mercy to others, as Jesus shed His blood for us.

I pray that the Holy Spirit will magnify the words in this book—that He will transform your vision, your heart, and your life of service to the King of kings. My hope is that you will stand before the King one day and receive the *crown of life* that awaits the faithful servant of God.

May the Lord bless you and keep you on the straight and narrow path that leads to life everlasting, and may you richly bless others as you walk the way of the cross.
Amen.

For ministry information:
Connie Cenac
9570 Regency Square Boulevard
Jacksonville, FL 32225 connie@hcmcinc.com